The
Breeze of the
Centuries

To my dear parents
This book is all about Exodus 20:12

For related resources, visit
www.great-theologians.org

Michael Reeves

The Breeze of the Centuries

•• Introducing great theologians ••
From the Apostolic Fathers to Aquinas

Inter-Varsity Press
Norton Street, Nottingham NG7 3HR, England
Email: ivp@ivpbooks.com
Website: www.ivpbooks.com

First published 2010

British Library Cataloguing in Publication Data
A catalogue record for this book is available from the British Library.

ISBN: 978-1-84474-415-2

Set in Garamond 11/13pt
Typeset in Great Britain by Servis Filmsetting Ltd, Stockport, Cheshire
Printed and bound in Great Britain by Ashford Colour Press Ltd, Gosport, Hampshire

Inter-Varsity Press publishes Christian books that are true to the Bible and that communicate the gospel, develop discipleship and strengthen the church for its mission in the world.

Inter-Varsity Press is closely linked with the Universities and Colleges Christian Fellowship, a student movement connecting Christian Unions in universities and colleges throughout Great Britain, and a member movement of the International Fellowship of Evangelical Students. Website: www.uccf.org.uk.

CONTENTS

ACKNOWLEDGMENTS

For four years now, I have had the enormous privilege of teaching theology to the staff of the Universities and Colleges Christian Fellowship. A more sparky bunch I have hardly known: they are living proof of how theology fires mission. It was they who first listened as I introduced them to these theologians, and who pondered with me as we applied old insights to today. I am filled with gratitude for them.

The other main force behind these volumes, to whom I owe a special word of thanks, is Dr Philip Duce at Inter-Varsity Press, a kind and deft editor without whom I would have been more than normally helpless.

I must also thank Professor John Webster, who inspired the project; the late Professor Colin Gunton, who shared with me his mercurial inquisitiveness and love for theology and Irenaeus; Dr Paul Melankreos, whose insights into the early post-apostolic church were invaluable; Professor Thomas Williams, who dispensed advice so willingly; Daniel Hames, who kept throwing fuel on the fire; Elizabeth Fraser, who suggested including timelines; Edward Coombs, who believed that heroes of the faith can still teach and inspire a Sunday congregation; and, above all, my dear wife, Bethan, for having the patience of Job.

INTRODUCTION: SNOBS, BUMPKINS AND DINOSAURS

C. S. Lewis was a self-confessed dinosaur. He knew perfectly well that he simply did not belong in the modern world. Yet, being born out of due time, he was able to spot what the natives could not. And what he saw in modern culture, perhaps more than anything else, was a suffocating enslavement to the beautiful myth of progress, the dream that history is evolving ever onwards and upwards, that newer is better.

It is the sort of belief that sits very comfortably in the subconscious, giving one the warm glow of knowing that we are faster, better, wiser, more advanced and more knowledgeable than our parents and forebears. Yet one of the problems Lewis noticed in the myth was that such superiority tends to produce not wisdom but ignorance. If we assume that the past is inferior, we will not bother consulting it, and will thus find ourselves stranded on the tiny desert island of our moment in time. Or, as Lewis put it, we will become like the country bumpkin, full of

the cocksure conviction of an ignorant adolescent that his own village (which is the only one he knows) is the hub of the universe and does everything in the Only Right Way. For our own age, with all its accepted ideas, stands to the vast extent of historical time much as one village stands to the whole world.[1]

Of course, such 'chronological snobbery' does not like to admit its own existence. No snob likes to be thought of as an ignorant bumpkin. Indeed, the chronological snob will often be the first to bedeck himself with historical references. The modern writer will allude to the old. But so often it is simply a case of the living plundering the dead. The cachet of the Augustine, the Luther, the Aquinas is purloined, as sound bites from their writings are torn from their original context and pressed into the service of other arguments, or simply used as weapons in the latest theological street fight.

But what Lewis found – and what reading old books makes very clear – is that every age works with a large set of assumptions that seem to it so self-evident they are never questioned. Like the proverbial frog in the kettle, we find it almost impossible to get a real sense of the water we inhabit, and can thus be blissfully unaware of how faddish our beliefs are. It is very tempting for me now to don the grand airs of a sage cultural critic and attempt to list what our unquestioned assumptions are today. But anyone excavating this book from the dusty bowels of some copyright library in fifty years' time would only chuckle at the profound issues I had overlooked. They are simply part of the air we breathe every day, and as such are quite invisible to us.

What to do? 'The only palliative', said Lewis, 'is to keep the clean sea breeze of the centuries blowing through our minds.'[2] That is, we refuse to imprison ourselves in the stuffy broom cupboard of the present and safely familiar, and open up the doors to the refreshing influences of other times. And practically?

---

1. C. S. Lewis, *Studies in Medieval and Renaissance Literature* (Cambridge: Cambridge University Press, 1966), p. 138.

2. C. S. Lewis, Introduction to *On the Incarnation* by Athanasius (London: Centenary, 1944; repr. Crestwood, N. Y.: SVS, 1998), p. 5.

It is a good rule, after reading a new book, never to allow yourself
another new one till you have read an old one in between. If that is too
much for you, you should at least read one old one to every three new
ones . . . Not, of course, that there is any magic about the past. People
were no cleverer then than they are now; they made as many mistakes
as we. But not the *same* mistakes. They will not flatter us in the errors
we are already committing; and their own errors, being now open and
palpable, will not endanger us. Two heads are better than one, not
because either is infallible, but because they are unlikely to go wrong in
the same direction. To be sure, the books of the future would be just as
good a corrective as the books of the past, but unfortunately we cannot
get at them.[3]

Such is the motivation behind *The Breeze of the Centuries* and its
companion volume. It is that, far from turning us into *irrelevant*
dinosaurs, reading old books can rescue us from bumpkinery and
enlarge our vision. From other centuries we receive an enrichment
we could never have through mere feeding on ourselves. And if
that is true for old books in general, it is more so for the books of
old theologians. Theology is something to be done corporately,
by the church. But if we ignore what the bulk of the church has
said down through history, then we act as schismatically as if we
ignored the church on earth today. More so, in fact.

Would Lewis not be appalled?

Clearly, then, this is a work built on Lewis's foundations. And
yet, is this not exactly the sort of dreary modern book Lewis
feared would insulate people from the health-giving breeze? Why
write another new book when the aim is to have people read old
ones?

But this was just why Lewis wrote so much. The fact is, theologians like Athanasius and Calvin are like famous guests of honour
at a party. Most people there would love to have some time with

---

3. Ibid., pp. 4–5.

them, but few dare to approach them without a polite introduction. And providing a few introductions to fascinating but
potentially intimidating celebrity theologians is the aim of these
pages.

In that sense, while there might seem to be an insane arrogance
to the thought of trying to squeeze such titans into so few pages,
this is actually a work that makes no great pretences. Rather, it
seeks to do itself out of a job by leading readers on to better books
than this. For that reason I will not spend time pontificating on
'Anselm's view of God' or 'Barth's view of Scripture' – to do so
could leave readers just as frightened of approaching the great
men for themselves, perhaps more so. Instead, I will try to intrude
as little as possible, simply letting the reader get to know the
theologians on their own terms. Of course, that will not be entirely
possible – and there will be moments when I will be unable to
restrain myself from commenting – but that is the aim: not to pre-
digest, pillage or spin, but to introduce real people, which means
people whose thoughts are so often a puzzling swirl of glories and
gaffes.

Reading these introductions

Each introduction will begin with a little biography and back-
ground – after all, no theology is written in a vacuum, and
somehow, knowing about, say, Athanasius' sense of humour and
his 'Boy's Own' adventures makes Athanasius easier to get into.
Then on to the theology, which will amount to a fast jog through
each theologian's major work(s). Note: this is rather different to
my writing on 'Calvin's doctrine of election' or the like; instead,
I will try to walk with readers through Calvin's *Institutes*, getting
to know its structure, feel and argument. Readers interested in
Calvin's doctrine of election should then feel confident enough
to put Reeves on one side and converse with Calvin direct. At the
end of each introduction I will make some suggestions for getting
to know that theologian better, and I will provide a timeline to
help give a snapshot-sense of the order and context of the life in
question.

There is a story that emerges from these pages, and readers who work through one introduction after another should, by the end of the second volume, have glimpsed something of the overall movement and flow of Christian thought through the centuries. However, this is just as much a work to dip in and out of. Its purpose is not so much to tell a grand narrative as to meet and get to know some of the key characters. And those characters are remarkably diverse: some will sound more winning, more trustworthy or more familiar; others may seem quite alien or off-putting. Thus if you find yourself floundering or overly enraged by one theologian, feel happy to move on to the next. He will, assuredly, be quite different.

But why these theologians, and not others? Quite simply, the goal of this work is to make accessible what otherwise seems intimidating, but if the very girth of the volumes was daunting, it would have failed in what it set out to do. I have therefore had to pick and choose theologians to introduce, and that means disappointing those whose heroes are not included. Still, I have not simply come up with a list of personal favourites; I have minor disagreements with every theologian here, and major problems with a few. Nor is this my list of 'great Christians'. Francis of Assisi, John Bunyan and John Wesley will make no appearance, though undoubtedly they were great and influential; it is that their greatness was not so much *as theologians*. Rather, I have tried to choose theologians who are influential or significant especially for the English-speaking world (many of whom, I suspect, are the very ones English-speaking people are most eager to know better). As a result, such mighty names as Origen, Palamas, Gerhard, Turretin and Suárez (the list could go on) are not included. My apologies to any who miss them: accessibility calls.

The last word of introduction really belongs to C. S. Lewis, who grasped so well the point of wrestling with theology:

> For my own part I tend to find the doctrinal books often more helpful
> in devotion than the devotional books, and I rather suspect that the
> same experience may await many others. I believe that many who find
> that 'nothing happens' when they sit down, or kneel down, to a book
> of devotion, would find that the heart sings unbidden while they are

working their way through a tough bit of theology with a pipe in their teeth and a pencil in their hand.[4]

May it be so for you now.

---

4. Ibid., p. 8.

1. ONLY LET ME REACH JESUS CHRIST!
The Apostolic Fathers

By the end of the first century AD, Jesus' apostles were all dead and Jerusalem and its temple had been destroyed. It was a crucial time of transition for Christianity, made all the more difficult by the hostile notice the Roman Empire began to pay as it saw what looked to it like a subversive new sect in its midst.

The writings of the Apostolic Fathers are the most important books for understanding those first generations after the apostles: how they thought, lived and died. The collection of the Apostolic Fathers consists of about ten authors who wrote from around the end of the first century to the middle of the second, put together by scholars and termed the Apostolic Fathers. However, as a group they are a real mixed bag: some are works by eminent figures of the time such as Polycarp of Smyrna; others are anonymous; they come from different genres (letters, works of apologetics, a sermon, an apocalypse, an account of a martyrdom, instructions on church order); and they represent a wide diversity of theologies. Perhaps the best way to understand them is to see them not as the best theology of the time, but as representative best-sellers of the generation after the apostles. As such they are not only significant but instructive.

We will examine each of the works normally included in the collection in order to see what they say and also to see what they tell us about earliest post-apostolic Christianity and its theology.

Papias

According to tradition, Papias, the bishop of Hierapolis in Asia Minor, was the disciple of the apostle John who actually wrote out John's Gospel as the apostle dictated it. He wrote a five-volume work of his own, *An Exposition of the Sayings of the Lord*; however, today only fragments of his work survive. During the second century, Papias was widely held in high esteem; yet, largely because of his characteristically second-century belief in a literal, future millennium, he fell out of favour with subsequent generations who tended to understand the millennium more symbolically. The great third- to fourth-century church historian Eusebius dismissed Papias for this reason as 'a man of exceedingly small intelligence'.[1]

Papias is valuable today for one reason in particular: he demonstrates for us the importance of oral tradition for early post-apostolic Christianity. It is clear from what survives of his work that an enormous number of oral traditions were in circulation concerning the life and sayings of Jesus and his apostles. It is also clear that such oral traditions were by no means distrusted as mere hearsay; instead, they were valued because they could be probed easily for veracity. For instance, Papias records that John and Philip went to evangelize Asia Minor, Philip settling with his family in Papias' own town of Hierapolis (where, according to tradition, Philip was martyred). John, he tells us, settled in Ephesus, was then exiled for a while to the island of Patmos, was recalled by the emperor Nerva (ad 96–8), whence he returned to Ephesus, there to be killed as the last of the apostles, in fulfilment of Mark

---

1. Eusebius, *Church History* 3.39; quoted from *Nicene and Post-Nicene Fathers*, Second Series, tr. P. Schaff and H. Wace, 14 vols. (Grand Rapids: Eerdmans, 1986–9).

10:38–39. Mark, he tells us, wrote his Gospel based on Peter's testimony (Mark being Peter's disciple and companion in Rome [1 Pet. 5:13]). If true, it adds an exquisite poignancy to Mark's graphic account of Peter's betrayal of Jesus. Papias' most gruesomely fascinating account, though, is of Judas. Papias believed that the two New Testament accounts of Judas' end (Matt. 27:3–10; Acts 1:15–9) could be harmonized by understanding that Judas did not die by hanging himself, but was cut down before he choked to death. Then he lived on, only to die when falling, so bloated that he burst open:

> Judas was a terrible, walking example of ungodliness in this world, his flesh so bloated that he was not able to pass through a place where a wagon passes easily, not even his bloated head by itself. For his eyelids, they say, were so swollen that he could not see the light at all, and his eyes could not be seen, even by a doctor using an optical instrument, so far had they sunk below the outer surface. His genitals appeared more loathsome and larger than anyone else's, and when he relieved himself there passed through it pus and worms from every part of his body, much to his shame. After much agony and punishment, they say, he finally died in his own place, and because of the stench the area is deserted and uninhabitable even now; in fact, to this day one cannot pass that place without holding one's nose, so great was the discharge from his body, and so far did it spread over the ground.[2]

Clement of Rome

1 Clement

Perhaps the oldest complete work in the collection, written around AD 95, is an anonymous letter traditionally attributed to Clement, Paul's co-worker (Phil. 4:3) and the third bishop of Rome after Peter. It was written to the ever-problematic church of Corinth in order to address a number of issues that were causing disquiet

---

2. A fragment of Papias' *Exposition of the Sayings of the Lord*, cited by Apollinaris of Laodicea.

there. One of those issues was still the resurrection of the body: the Corinthians clearly had not taken the message of 1 Corinthians 15 to heart! The main problem, however, was that the old concern of disunity had led to the church's elders being ousted in a church coup and replaced.

1 Clement argues that the takeover was entirely wrong, being motivated by pride and greed, and that the ousted elders must be restored. According to the letter, the move was a rebellion against God, who has appointed a proper ecclesiastical order: God commissioned Christ, who commissioned apostles, who commissioned bishops, who commission deacons.[3] It is arguable whether or not this is a reference to the doctrine of apostolic succession as it would come to be formulated (after all, here the elders were said to have been appointed 'with the consent of the whole church'[4]). What is clear, though, is that the role of the church elder has a significance in *1 Clement* that it does not have in 1 Corinthians: church unity now seems to be sought more in the elders than in the Spirit.

Advocates of Episcopal church government argue that *1 Clement* is evidence of a very early and natural evolution of episcopalism. The fact that Clement was himself bishop of Rome is also used by advocates of papal supremacy to support their theory by suggesting that he wrote with authority to another church because of his position, even though there is no internal evidence in the letter to suggest this.

At the other end of the interpretative spectrum are those who see an almost complete discontinuity between a New Testament radical congregationalism and a monarchical episcopalism in the next generation. On this reading, earliest apostolic Christianity had no concept of eldership, churches being charismatic communities with no need for such leadership, meaning that the pastoral epistles (1 and 2 Timothy and Titus) must be dismissed as later

---

3. *1 Clement* 42.
4. Ibid. 44.3. All Apostolic Fathers quotations from here on are from Michael Holmes's translation, *The Apostolic Fathers in English*, 3rd ed. (Grand Rapids: Baker, 2006).

'deutero-Pauline' books because of their concern for church offices. Stimulating this kind of interpretation was a seminal work published in 1934 by Walter Bauer entitled *Orthodoxy and Heresy in Earliest Christianity*. Bauer's claim was that an originally diverse Christianity soon began to be dominated by just one authoritarian group, found in Rome. The Roman church then rewrote history, setting its own beliefs as the standard of orthodoxy and labelling all dissent as heresy. Bauer's thesis was seriously flawed (if power bought the title 'orthodox', how could those emperors who were Arian be dismissed as heretics?), yet it initiated what is today a prolific trend for describing orthodoxy as mere authoritarianism.[5]

2 Clement

The second letter of Clement is misleadingly titled: it is neither a letter, nor is it by Clement. It is a sermon, quite possibly preached by one of the Corinthian elders who were restored to their offices following Clement's 'first' letter. The sermon has to do with a call to repentance, to think of Christ as God and to believe in the resurrection. Its greatest value for us, though, is probably its treatment of Scripture: it contains the earliest example (outside the New Testament) of a passage from the New Testament being referred to as 'Scripture' alongside the Old Testament.[6] It reveals that there was a clear and early understanding of a New Testament canon of Scripture.

Ignatius of Antioch

One of the most remarkable and memorable figures of the first post-apostolic generation was Ignatius, bishop of Antioch in Syria. Strangely, we know almost nothing about him until he explodes on to the historical scene just a few weeks before his martyrdom in around AD 110. During a citywide persecution, he and some other Christians were arrested and sent to Rome to be thrown to wild

---

5. Bart Ehrman is perhaps the foremost exponent of this view today.
6. *2 Clement* 2.4.

beasts in the arena. En route, under armed guard, he dashed off seven letters to the churches he would pass through: the churches of Ephesus, Magnesia, Tralles, Philadelphia, Smyrna (as well as one to Polycarp, the bishop of Smyrna), and Rome. The letters really were dashed off (their style shows that they were written hastily and under considerable strain); nevertheless, they make for fascinating and illuminating reading. They are the last words of a man with only weeks to live, and yet, to quote Bruce Metzger, are filled with 'such strong faith and overwhelming love of Christ as to make them one of the finest literary expressions of Christianity during the second century'.[7]

As he wrote, Ignatius had three main concerns on his mind. The first was that the churches be unified under their respective bishops. On this issue, Ignatius is so strongly Episcopalian he makes Clement appear positively Congregationalist in contrast. For Ignatius, the church finds its unity through the bishop, and therefore he writes, 'you must not do anything without the bishop and the presbyters'; indeed, it 'is not permissible either to baptize or to hold a love feast without the bishop'.[8] This is because, for Ignatius, the bishop represents Christ to the church, and thus to meet without the bishop would be to fail to be Christ's church: 'For everyone whom the Master of the house sends to manage his own house we must welcome as we would the one who sent him. It is obvious, therefore, that we must regard the bishop as the Lord himself.'[9]

The second concern on Ignatius' mind was the problem of false teaching. In particular, Ignatius had two types of false teachers in mind: Docetists and Judaizers, both of whom denied in their own way that Christ had come in the flesh (cf. 1 John).

The Docetists maintained that Jesus was entirely divine, and that he only *appeared* to be human (the name 'Docetic' comes from the Greek word *dokeō*, meaning 'to seem' or 'to appear'). Perhaps

---

7. B. M. Metzger, *The Canon of the New Testament: Its Origin, Development, and Significance* (Oxford: Clarendon, 1987), p. 44.

8. *Magnesians* 7.1; *Smyrnaeans* 8.2. Quotations are taken from Holmes, *Apostolic Fathers in English*.

9. *Ephesians* 6.1; cf. *Trallians* 3.1; *Ephesians* 5.3; *Smyrnaeans* 6.2.

the most notorious Docetic teacher was Marcion, who taught that the good Saviour-God of the New Testament is a different being to the bad Creator-God of the Old Testament. Jesus thus had nothing to do with the evil Creator-God's physical world, and so could not actually have had a physical body, been born, have eaten, died and so on. In stark opposition, Ignatius would boldly speak of 'the blood of God', for if the divine Christ had not truly assumed our humanity, then he could not have died for our sins.[10] In fact, Ignatius' entire motivation in accepting martyrdom was based upon his belief in the real incarnation of Christ: Ignatius longed for martyrdom because then he would be copying Christ, but if Christ did not really suffer in his body, then Ignatius could not be copying him at all. 'If that is the case, I die for no reason,' he wrote.[11] Instead, Ignatius wanted his life and death to proclaim that 'There is only one physician, who is both flesh and spirit, born and unborn, God in man, true life in death, both from Mary and from God, first subject to suffering and then beyond it, Jesus Christ our Lord.'[12] It is hard to read such material and not be incredulous of the claim that Jesus' full divinity and full humanity is a later, fourth-century invention.

The other type of false teacher Ignatius was eager to arm Christians against (particularly in Magnesia and Philadelphia) was the Judaizer, who taught that Christians must abide by Jewish customs, especially circumcision and the Mosaic Law. For a time when Christianity was only just beginning to be recognized as something distinct from Judaism, this was a most pressing issue. Ignatius argued that the Judaizer's teaching misunderstood the very nature of the Old Testament: 'if we continue to live in accordance with Judaism, we admit that we have not received grace. For the most godly prophets lived in accordance with Christ Jesus.'[13] The mistake of the Judaizers was to fail to see that Old Testament believers were themselves Christians, saved by nothing else than

---

10. *Ephesians* 1.1; cf. *Romans* 6.3.

11. *Trallians* 10.1; cf. *Smyrnaeans* 4.2.

12. *Ephesians* 7.2.

13. *Magnesians* 8.1–2; cf. 9.2.

by trusting in Christ.[14] The Jewish Scriptures existed to proclaim
Christ and his gospel. As we will see, this was to be the issue of
issues for many Christians of the day, who saw that the entire
legitimacy of their faith depended on the Hebrew Scriptures
being inherently Christian. If they were not, then Judaism, not
Christianity, was true.

Ignatius' third concern as he wrote his letters was, understandably, his own death. This surfaces most clearly in his letter to the
Romans. The point of his letter is to beg the Christians in Rome
not to try to help him escape death when he arrives, for he is eager
to be martyred:

> I implore you: do not be unseasonably kind to me. Let me be food for
> the wild beasts . . . Bear with me – I know what is best for me. Now at
> last I am beginning to be a disciple. May nothing visible or invisible envy
> me, so that I may reach Jesus Christ. Fire and cross and battles with wild
> beasts, mutilation, mangling, wrenching of bones, the hacking of limbs,
> the crushing of my whole body, cruel tortures of the devil – let these
> come upon me, only let me reach Jesus Christ![15]

This enthusiasm of his is so inexplicable to many modern commentators that he is all too often written off as a psychotic. In
point of fact, however, he is profoundly realistic, anticipating, for
example, that his courage may well fail when the moment comes.
Thus he writes, 'if upon my arrival I myself should appeal to you,
do not be persuaded by me'.[16] Part of Ignatius' reasoning was that
Christians were normally only released upon denying Christ, and
this would undoubtedly be what people would assume had happened if Ignatius were released, even if the Roman church really
did manage to secure his freedom in another way. He would rather
suffer death than that. Far more significantly, though, Ignatius
believed that the best way for him to follow Christ was through
the same kind of violent death Christ had suffered. In this way he

---

14. *Philadelphians* 9.1.
15. *Romans* 4.1; 5.3.
16. Ibid. 7.2.

would become most Christlike, and thus most clearly confess the saving suffering of his God.[17]

Polycarp of Smyrna

Ignatius sent one of his letters to Polycarp, the bishop of Smyrna and former disciple of the apostle John, who is probably the most renowned of all the Apostolic Fathers because of the martyrdom he would also suffer.

The Letter of Polycarp to the Philippians

Polycarp himself wrote a letter to the church of Philippi a few weeks after Ignatius' death in order to tackle some difficulties they were facing. The presenting issue was that one of their elders, Valens, had embezzled some of the church funds.[18] However, there was also a problem of false teaching. When Paul wrote to the Philippians sixty or so years earlier, he had had to tackle some Judaizing false teachers (Phil. 3:2–3). By Polycarp's time, the false teaching was more predominately Docetic.[19] What is perhaps most interesting about Polycarp's letter is the mildness of his rebuke to Valens in comparison with his treatment of the false teachers. Valens, who had been immoral, is called to repentance; the false teachers, on the other hand, are anathematized as 'the firstborn of Satan'.[20] What appears to be going on is that Polycarp viewed theological belief as the impetus for behaviour, and thus wrong belief would corrupt and splinter the church. The church in this harassed time needed to stand fast in its doctrine in order to stand fast at all.

The Martyrdom of Polycarp

The eyewitness account of the events leading up to, and including, Polycarp's execution fill out for us our understanding of both

---

17. Ibid. 6.3.
18. *Philippians* 11.1.
19. Ibid. 6.3 – 7.1.
20. Ibid. 11.4; 7.1.

the post-apostolic church's theology of martyrdom, and of why Christians of the time were persecuted.

The account describes Polycarp's martyrdom as the last in a local wave of persecution. Thus it begins with the trials and martyrdoms of other local Christians. Most are said to have been given extraordinary courage in their moment of need. However, one man, Quintus, rashly volunteered himself for martyrdom, only to apostatize when threatened. His behaviour is included as a warning not to volunteer for martyrdom, however good it might be for those on whom it is thrust (like Ignatius).[21]

Polycarp is then sought out, and neither seeks martyrdom nor shies away from it. From then on, numerous parallels between the last hours of Christ and Polycarp show Polycarp to be an exemplary follower of Christ. Like Ignatius, he is being a disciple in facing his martyrdom. The Roman officials try to persuade Polycarp to say 'Caesar is Lord', to offer him incense and to revile Christ. He continually refuses (at which time he utters the immortal words 'eighty-six years I have been his [Christ's] servant, and he has done me no wrong. How can I blaspheme my King who saved me?'[22]), and eventually he is sentenced to be burned at the stake. The fire, however, fails to kill Polycarp, and thus he is stabbed to death.

We can learn a number of things from the account. We see that it was the mob, rather than the government, that instigated a local persecution of the Christians. This was certainly the normal pattern: there were instances when systematic persecution became Roman imperial policy,[23] but by and large persecution was popularly motivated, and thus sporadic and local. We also see that the reason Christians were persecuted was not per se because they were Christian, but because they refused to worship the state gods,

---

21. *Martyrdom* 4.
22. Ibid. 9.3.
23. This happened during the reigns of the emperors Nero (54–68), Trajan (98–117), Marcus Aurelius (161–80), Septimius Severus (193–211), Maximian (235), Decius and Valerian (249–60) and Diocletian and Galerian (303–13).

especially the emperor. To refuse to worship the emperor looked seditious to the Roman mind, for which religion was a highly political concept; to fail to worship the other gods looked dangerously anti-social, for the gods, if not revered, could mete out all manner of punishments from plague to crop failure. For the people, the persecution of such blasphemers was self-protection. It was for this reason that, a generation later, the great African theologian Tertullian wrote:

> If the Tiber rises as high as the city walls, if the Nile does not send its waters up over the fields, if the heavens give no rain, if there is an earthquake, if there is famine or pestilence, straightway the cry is, 'Away with the Christians to the lion!'[24]

The Didache

The Didache (teaching) *of the Apostles* was a work known only by its title until its discovery, amid much media excitement, in a library in Constantinople in 1873. Its discovery caused such a stir because it is such an early (c. AD 100) and detailed discussion of life, practice and beliefs in the early post-apostolic church.

It starts with a section of ethical teaching, explaining that there are two paths for us, the path of life (an extremely strict code of morality) and the path of death (failure to adhere to that code). What is both striking and disturbing is that there is nothing explicitly Christian in that entire section of ethical instruction. Justification and the gospel of grace are poignantly absent, leaving the impression of a life that knows far more of legalism than freedom. Ironically, it feels a very far cry from the actual teaching of the apostles as we have it in the New Testament. Instead, being so early an exhibit of Christian legalism, it serves as a powerful affirmation of the apostle Paul's point, that people can turn with astonishing speed from the grace of Christ to another gospel (Gal. 1:6).

---

24. Tertullian, *Apology* 40.

The next section gives instructions on how to practise baptism, prayer, fasting and the Eucharist, before moving on to deal with what was evidently a growing problem: what to do with itinerant 'apostles and prophets'. Apparently, two types of Christian leader had developed by this time: itinerant prophets who followed the apostle Paul's model of ministry, and local church elders who were permanent members of one church. The problem, however, was that, unlike Paul, some of these prophets had begun to be a burden to local churches by living off them. While respecting the office of the itinerant prophet as of equal value to that of the elder, *The Didache* responds with strict instructions on how to sort out the rogues: if, for example, they stay for more than two days, order meals 'in the spirit' or ask for money, they are to be rejected as false prophets.[25]

The work closes with a brief apocalyptic section, which is just one of many reminders in the Apostolic Fathers that the future return of Christ was an almost shockingly prominent feature in the minds of that generation of Christians. It forcefully moulded not only how they died, but also how they lived.

The Shepherd of Hermas

The most popular and influential of the Apostolic Fathers in its day was the lengthy quasi-apocalyptic book *The Shepherd of Hermas*. In it the author (Hermas) records in floridly religious tones a number of visions he has received concerning the nature and state of the church in his day. For the first half of the book, these visions are interpreted to him by a female figure who represents the church. In the second half of the book it is Hermas' guardian angel who interprets the visions to him while taking the form of a shepherd (hence the title of the book).

Hermas begins the work by writing of a time when he had lusted after a woman he once saw bathing in the river Tiber. His first vision then commences, in which he sees the woman

---

25. *Didache* 11.5–6.

accusing him from heaven. At first, surprisingly, he is surprised, and responds, 'I sinned against you? In what way? Or when have I ever spoken an indecent word to you? Have I not always regarded you as a goddess?' (not the best defence, one might have thought, though he certainly had thought about her like this when he saw her naked in the river).[26] Yet she convinces him that his lust was sin, leaving him to wonder, 'If even this sin is recorded against me, how can I be saved? Or how will I propitiate God for my conscious sins?'[27] This sets the scene for the rest of the book, which is chiefly concerned with the possibility of forgiveness.

Four more visions follow, the most important of which concerns a tower built on water.[28] This represents the church built on baptism and reveals what a high view of baptism had started to emerge in certain Christian circles. It begins to clarify a main concern of the book, and what was clearly a popular concern of the day: is there a possibility of forgiveness after the washing of baptism? The answer given is yes, but only one possibility, for 'there is only one repentance for God's servants'.[29] It was this graceless belief that fuelled the practice of postponing baptism until near death. The sorts of things Hermas sees in the vision are angelic builders removing stones from the tower, indicating the removal of believers for sin, and round stones that do not fit, representing rich believers, who must first have their riches chopped away before they can fit into the tower.[30]

Next come twelve 'commandments', all largely pragmatic and moral. The sixth contains the crudest statement of salvation by works prior to the arch-heretic Pelagius:

'Now hear,' he said, 'about faith. There are two angels with a person, one of righteousness and one of wickedness . . . This commandment explains the things about faith, in order that you may trust the works of the angel

---

26. *Hermas* 1.7.
27. Ibid. 2.1.
28. Ibid. 9–21.
29. Ibid. 29.8; 31.1–7.
30. Ibid. 13.5; 14.5–7.

of righteousness, and that doing them, you may live to God. But believe that the works of the angel of wickedness are dangerous, so that by not doing them you will live to God.'[31]

Surely the oddest commandment, though, is the tenth:

> Clothe yourself, therefore, with cheerfulness, which always finds favor with God and is acceptable to him, and rejoice in it. For all cheerful people do good things and think good things, and despise grief. But sorrowful people always do evil.[32]

One wonders how the apostle Paul would have reacted (cf. Rom. 9:2), for this is nothing like his liberating theology of joy.

The book ends with ten 'parables', or lessons to be learned from trees, vines, stones and so on. These too contain 'wisdom' that seems almost entirely ignorant of salvation not by merit but by grace:

> Keep the Lord's commandments, and you will be pleasing to him and will be enrolled among the number of those who keep his commandments. But if you do anything good beyond God's commandment, you will gain greater glory for yourself, and will be more honored in God's sight than you otherwise would have been.[33]

The idea that we can do good works above and beyond what God commands ('works of supererogation') was wholly rejected by Protestants at the time of the Reformation as an arrogant undermining of both man's sinful inability before God, and God's grace.[34] Yet it fits Hermas' understanding that the gospel is a new

---

31. Ibid. 36.1, 10.
32. Ibid. 42.1–2.
33. Ibid. 56.2–3.
34. Article 14 of the Church of England's Thirty-Nine Articles, for
    example, reads, 'Voluntary Works besides, over and above, God's
    Commandments, which they call Works of Supererogation, cannot be
    taught without arrogancy and impiety: for by them men do declare, that

law from God.[35] On this understanding, it is no wonder that mere faith is insufficient to be justified before God. In this way *The Shepherd of Hermas* is the most stark indication of a popular turn in the early second century from the gospel of grace to a harsh legalism.

Letter to Diognetus

The final two Apostolic Fathers are essentially works of apologetics. They are the *Letter of Barnabas*, a work that seeks to defend Christianity in the face of Judaism, and the *Letter to Diognetus*, a piece that defends Christianity in the face of paganism.

Apologies became a popular form of literature among Christians in the second century, both because of the desire to promote Christianity, and because of the need to defend it from often-violent attack. Other examples include the *Octavius* of Minucius Felix and the works of Justin Martyr. In the *Octavius* we learn that Christians were accused by society at large of gross sexual immorality, incest, cannibalism and murder. Minucius Felix explains that these charges arose out of complete misunderstandings of the facts that Christians were compelled to meet secretly, where they would greet each other as brothers and sisters with the kiss of peace (whence the charges of incest), there to eat the flesh and drink the blood of the Son of God (whence the charges of cannibalism).

The *Letter to Diognetus* is a work nobody seemed to know of until a manuscript was discovered in 1436, being used to wrap fish in a fishmonger's shop in Constantinople![36] It is an anonymous work, though it is possible that it could be either the lost apology of

---

they do not only render unto God as much as they are bound to do, but that they do more for his sake, than of bounden duty is required: whereas Christ saith plainly, When ye have done all that are commanded to you, say, We are unprofitable servants.'

35. *Hermas* 69.2.

36. The manuscript fared little better later on; having been transcribed, it was

Quadratus spoken of by Eusebius,[37] or by Polycarp. It is addressed to a 'most excellent Diognetus', who could well be the Diognetus who was a tutor to the emperor Marcus Aurelius, making it most likely that the work was intended as an open letter for public consumption by a pagan audience.

Apparently, Diognetus had expressed interest in why Christians worshipped neither the gods of the pagans, nor in the same way as the Jews. The author replies with an attack on idolatry that is reminiscent of Isaiah 44: the gods of wood and stone are deaf, dumb and blind. 'These are the things you call gods; you serve them, you worship them, and in the end you become like them.'[38] It is a mocking but deftly made theological point: we become like the gods we serve.

The Jews, he goes on to argue, are equally mistaken in their understanding of God, for, as pagans make offerings to gods unable to receive them, so Jews make offerings to God when in fact he has no need of them.[39] This argument fits well into an understanding of the gospel that is refreshingly opposed to the legalism of *The Didache* and *The Shepherd of Hermas*. In fact, reading the *Letter to Diognetus* is like reading Luther in comparison. For example, he writes of God that

> when our unrighteousness was fulfilled, and it had been made perfectly
> clear that its wages – punishment and death – were to be expected
> . . . he himself gave up his own Son as a ransom for us, the holy one
> for the lawless, the guiltless for the guilty, the just for the unjust, the
> incorruptible for the corruptible, the immortal for the mortal. For what

---

Footnote 36 (*cont.*)
   destroyed when the library of Strasbourg, where it had been deposited, was bombed in 1870.
37. A fragment from the apology of Quadratus, preserved for us by Eusebius (*Church History* 4.3.1–2), is sometimes included in the collection of the Apostolic Fathers. Some scholars believe that the fragment should be fitted into a gap that exists in the text of the *Letter to Diognetus*.
38. *Diognetus* 2.5.
39. Ibid. 3.5.

else but his righteousness could have covered our sins? In whom was it possible for us, the lawless and ungodly, to be justified, except in the Son of God alone? O the sweet exchange, O the incomprehensible work of God, O the unexpected blessings, that the sinfulness of many should be hidden in one righteous person, while the righteousness of one should justify many sinners![40]

His argument continues with a defence of the innocence of Christians. Yet, he maintains, 'what the soul is to the body, Christians are to the world' – that is, as the soul is in the body but not of it, so Christians are in the world, and so, like souls, are despised. And, just as the soul is improved by fasting, so Christians increase when persecuted.[41]

Finally, amid an explanation of how God has shown his love to us sinners in sending Christ for our salvation, the author calls Diognetus to acquire the joyous knowledge of God for himself. 'Then you will admire those who for righteousness' sake endure the transitory fire, and you will consider them blessed, when you comprehend that other fire . . .'[42] Again the author makes it clear that the coming judgment was a prime consolation for the persecuted Christians of the time.

Letter of Barnabas

The last of the Apostolic Fathers is an anonymous letter, allegedly written by the apostle Paul's companion, Barnabas. It is often interpreted as an argument that the Christian church has superseded and replaced the Jewish nation as God's true people. However, it is in fact an argument that, from the very beginning, the faithful always were Christian, even though the majority of the nation of Israel failed to understand their own Scriptures' proclamation of Christ.

---

40. Ibid. 9.2–5.
41. Ibid. 6.
42. Ibid. 10.8.

Like Ignatius, Barnabas held that the Old Testament was originally intended as a Christian book. Both saw that unless the original authors of the Scriptures had intended to teach the Christian gospel, then Christians could validly be accused by Jews of reading an alien meaning back into those Scriptures. Yet, if a Christological understanding of the Old Testament were possible only with hindsight, Christianity could be neither authentic nor credible. In order to be able to face Judaism and Marcion alike, Barnabas argued that a true understanding of Moses should lead to faith in Christ.[43] Thus he writes, 'Abraham, who first instituted circumcision, looked forward in the spirit to Jesus when he circumcised';[44] Moses, both by stretching out his hands on the hill in Exodus 17, and by lifting up the serpent on the pole in Numbers 21, deliberately showed the people 'a symbol of Jesus'.[45] 'Again, what does Moses say to "Jesus" the son of Nun when he gave him this name, since he was a prophet, for the sole purpose that all the people might hear that the Father was revealing everything about his Son Jesus?'[46] Barnabas' intention is to demonstrate that Moses and the prophets were deliberate in prophesying Jesus' work. For this reason he does not appeal to the New Testament to support his argument (in any case, he could not, given that the New Testament was not yet a fixed canon), but seeks instead to interpret the Old Testament on its own terms so that his reading can be seen to represent the inherent meaning of the Hebrew Scriptures.

After looking at aspects of the sacrificial system, the events of the exodus and so on, Barnabas comes to consider Solomon's temple, and his treatment of it illustrates his entire approach. He argues that the temple in Jerusalem was an earthly copy that existed to proclaim a spiritual reality. The mistake of the Jews who

---

43. For a helpful discussion of how this principle functioned in the wider church at the time, see Gerald Bray, *Creeds, Councils and Christ*, 2nd ed. (Fearn: Mentor, 1997), pp. 49–54.

44. *Barnabas* 9.7.

45. Ibid. 12.5–6.

46. Ibid. 12.8.

set their hope on the building was to set their gaze on the copy, when they should have learnt about the spiritual reality from it.[47] So it was with circumcision and the entire law: the Jewish mistake was to confuse the earthly signs with the spiritual realities they represented. In looking only to the earthly, they found themselves enslaved to the ruler of this age and his angels.[48] And thus, by failing to be led to Christ by their own Scriptures, Barnabas maintains that Jews had come to worship a quite different god.

Barnabas' letter may not appear to cover material as urgently significant for the time as, say, a theology of martyrdom; however, what he makes clear is that the battle for Christianity's survival in the hostile second century was as much as anything else the battle for ownership of the Scriptures.

Going on with the Apostolic Fathers

In order to read the Apostolic Fathers themselves, the best place to start is probably with Michael Holmes's excellent modern translation, *The Apostolic Fathers in English*, 3rd ed. (Grand Rapids: Baker, 2006). Holmes also provides brief introductions to each work. After that, Clayton Jefford has provided the two most useful introductions: a shorter one, *The Apostolic Fathers: An Essential Guide* (Nashville: Abingdon, 2006), and a slightly longer one, *Reading the Apostolic Fathers* (Peabody: Hendrickson, 1996).

---

47. Ibid. 16.
48. Ibid. 18.1–2; 9.4.

Apostolic Fathers timeline

60–135?	Papias
64	Great Fire of Rome
64–8	Nero's punishment of the Christians
70	Destruction of the temple in Jerusalem
70–135	*Letter of Barnabas*
95?	*1 Clement*
96?	*2 Clement*
100?	*The Didache*
100–165	Justin Martyr
110?	Martyrdom of Ignatius
110–40?	*The Shepherd of Hermas*
130–200	Irenaeus of Lyons
150–90	*Letter to Diognetus*
155?	Martyrdom of Polycarp
160–225	Tertullian
303–12	The 'Great Persecution'
312	Conversion of the emperor Constantine to Christianity
325	Council of Nicea

2. TO ARMS
Justin Martyr and Irenaeus

By the second half of the second century AD, Christianity was despised by Judaism, feared by the official paganism of the Roman Empire, and infested with heresies. The need for theologians and apologists of substance was great. Many arose, but perhaps the greatest of these were Justin Martyr and Irenaeus.

Justin Martyr

Justin was born somewhere around AD 100 in Flavia Neapolis, where ancient Shechem had been and where Nablus is today, in Palestine. However, his family were probably Gentile pagans, rather than native Samaritans; certainly, he was given a Greek education. All this was an apt upbringing for a man who would go on to defend Christianity from both Jewish and cultured Greek attacks. Justin himself tells us that his education led him to dabble in some of the main branches of Greek philosophy: Stoicism, Peripateticism and Pythagoreanism, before becoming a settled Platonist.

At some point he moved to Ephesus, which is almost certainly where, struck by how fearlessly Christians died and sensing that here was the true and highest philosophy, he converted to Christianity. For the rest of his life he wore the gown traditionally donned by Greek philosophers in order to present Christianity as the goal of all searches for knowledge. Travelling widely, he visited Rome, where he lived near the Colosseum and founded a school of theology.

Justin wrote a number of works of theology and apologetics; however, today only three remain that scholars agree are authentically his. They are his *First* and *Second Apologies* and his *Dialogue with Trypho*.

First Apology

Justin's *First Apology* was written around AD 153–4 as an open letter to Emperor Antoninus Pius and his two adopted sons who would succeed him, Marcus Aurelius and Lucius Verus. All three were renowned as keen philosophers and just rulers, and it is to these traits that Justin appeals.

The *Apology* opens with a plea for Christians to be judged on the basis of evidence, and for charges against them to be investigated before judgment was passed. Clearly, the reality on the ground was that Christians were being punished on the basis of unsubstantiated rumours, the three main forms of which Justin goes on to counter. First, he states, Christians are not atheists as alleged, for they worship the Father, Son and Spirit. Secondly, Christians are not immoral, but are all prepared to stand proper trial for their conduct. Thirdly, they are not seditious, the kingdom they seek not being of this world. Rather, they are loyal citizens, paying their taxes.

Having thus dealt with the common charges against Christianity, Justin then goes on to show the positive value of Christianity. It is unreasonable to dismiss Christian beliefs, he argues, for they are the most reasonable. Many Christian beliefs, he suggests, share similarities with features of paganism that Romans happily accepted (the Romans believed in an afterlife, in deification [for Caesar at least][1] and in virgin birth [Perseus supposedly was born

---

1. It was common for theologians of the early post-apostolic church to speak of deification as a key aspect of Christian salvation. Quite different

of a virgin]). The difference is, Christians have concrete historical reasons for their belief, whereas pagans have nothing better than unsubstantiated fables.

The main bulk of Justin's argument, though, is taken up with addressing what was in its day perhaps the most fundamental objection to Christianity. In the second century and the centuries around it, antiquity was venerated and novelty despised. Thus Rome was generally tolerant towards the monotheism of Judaism that otherwise jarred so awkwardly with its own pluralism and imperial cult, but was intolerant towards what it saw in Christianity as an upstart sect. Justin's response is to argue that Christianity is, in fact, the oldest of religions. Christ's birth was predicted by Jacob (Gen. 49:10), Isaiah (7:14) and Micah (5:2), among others; his death was predicted by many (e.g. Ps. 22). And since they understood such things, believers such as Abraham were, in fact, Christians. The reason, he argues, why the Jews are not Christian is because they fail to understand their own Scriptures' witness to the Father and the Son, and the promise of Christ's coming. Worse, they even remove from their own Scriptures the verses that most offend them. An example he gives is Psalm 96:10, which he says should read 'the LORD has reigned from the tree', but from which the Jews had cut the words 'from the tree' because of its obvious reference to the cross.[2]

---

things could be meant by it. For theologians of the second century, though, deification was normally seen as being roughly synonymous with adoption; that is, through the Spirit, Christians are made sons of the Most High in the Firstborn Son, Christ (cf. *Dialogue with Trypho* 124). In this way, Christians can be said to enter the eternal fellowship of the Father, Son and Spirit.

2. *1 Apology* 41. We no longer have the edition of the psalm that Justin is referring to, though it seems unlikely that his argument came from a mere slip of the memory (he repeats the claim in his *Dialogue with Trypho* 73). A number of other theologians from the first five centuries AD also believed that Ps. 96:10 should read, 'the LORD has reigned from the tree' (cf. Tertullian, *An Answer to the Jews* 10, 13; *Five Books Against Marcion* 3.19; Augustine, Comment on Ps. 96).

Justin then goes on to argue that because Christianity is the oldest, rather than the latest, religion, ancient and venerated philosophers stole their best ideas from it. In particular, he argues, Plato plagiarized Moses in composing his philosophy. Moses, for instance, had created the tabernacle according to the heavenly pattern shown him on Mount Sinai; Plato had adapted this idea to suggest that all earthly things are copies of an ideal reality:

> And the physiological discussion concerning the Son of God in the *Timaeus* of Plato, where he says, 'He placed him crosswise in the universe,' he borrowed in like manner from Moses; for in the writings of Moses it is related how at that time, when the Israelites went out of Egypt and were in the wilderness, they fell in with poisonous beasts, both vipers and asps, and every kind of serpent, which slew the people; and that Moses, by the inspiration and influence of God, took brass, and made it into the figure of a cross . . . Which things Plato reading, and not accurately understanding, and not apprehending that it was the figure of the cross, but taking it to be a placing crosswise, he said that the power next to the first God was placed crosswise in the universe. And as to his speaking of a third, he did this because he read, as we said above, that which was spoken by Moses, 'that the Spirit of God moved over the waters.' For he gives the second place to the Logos which is with God, who he said was placed crosswise in the universe; and the third place to the Spirit who was said to be borne upon the water.[3]

And it was not just Plato who was guilty of plagiarism, according to Justin. The demons have always aped true religion in their attempt to lure humanity into idolatry. For instance, the idea of Bacchus, the God of wine, born out of the union of a God and a woman, and honoured in the drinking of wine, was stolen from Moses' prophecies of Christ and perverted.[4]

---

3. *1 Apology* 59.

4. Ibid. 69. Justin's argument here may seem very alien to us today; however, it is becoming relevant again as the old accusation resurfaces that Christianity has stolen its ideas from older sources. Rob Bell mentions precisely this example of Bacchus/Dionysus when he asks

Furthermore, Christ is the true Logos. All humans, he says, being 'logical' creatures, have something of the Logos in their nature (though he does not explicitly connect this with the image of God). When they speak proper logic, they speak of something the fullness of which is found in Christ. Thus Socrates, in upholding proper logic against all the false gods of classical Athens, could, on this basis, be said to have 'partially known' Christ.[5] Therefore, it is not just a question of plagiarism: the Christ-centred nature of reality, Christ being the Logos, means that human philosophy and mythology must necessarily contain echoes of the truth of the gospel. Yet those echoes are always so garbled, weak and self-contradictory that those who believe them are condemned out of their own mouths, for the echoes in themselves display their own futility.

Christianity, Justin thus concludes, is the true philosophy, and is therefore to be examined, respected and followed, not condemned.

Second Apology

Soon after Justin had finished writing his *First Apology*, three people were beheaded in Rome simply for confessing they were Christians. Justin hastily responded with an appendix to his work. We now refer to this addition as his *Second Apology*, even though it is not really a separate work.

Many of the same themes reappear, but Justin deals with two more popular objections to Christianity: (1) Since Christians seem to love martyrdom so much, why do they not all commit suicide? (2) Why does God not protect Christians? To the first he responds that, while Christians are happy to face death, they live for God's

---

if, hypothetically, 'the virgin birth was really just a bit of mythologizing the Gospel writers threw in to appeal to the followers of the Mithra and Dionysian religious cults that were hugely popular at the time of Jesus, whose gods had virgin births' (*Velvet Elvis: Repainting the Christian Faith* [Grand Rapids: Zondervan, 2005], p. 26). For Justin, the answer is simple: Christianity and the promise of a virgin birth is older than the Mithra and Dionysian cults; if anything, they stole from Christianity, not vice versa.

5. *2 Apology* 10; cf. *1 Apology* 46.

will, which is that they bring life to others. To the second he replies that evil angels cause suffering in the world, but that God allows it to discipline his beloved. He then turns the martyrdom objections into a challenge by arguing that the way Christians die is proof that Christianity has a truth which all the philosophies and superstitions of men do not have.

Dialogue with Trypho

Justin's last and most substantial work is another apology, this time written to answer the anti-Christian claims of Judaism. It takes the form of a two-day debate with an educated Jew (Trypho), often thought to be the great Rabbi Tarphon mentioned in the Mishnah. It is clearly not a stenographer's account, yet neither does it seem to be a mere literary device, as some more sceptical scholars would have it. It seems to be an account of an actual dialogue between Justin and Trypho.

The *Dialogue* is interesting for a number of reasons. First, we see how strongly trinitarian Justin is: he clearly sees the Father, Son and Spirit as three distinct persons.[6] Secondly, we are clearly shown the stark difference between the rabbinic Jewish reading of Scripture and the early post-apostolic Christian reading. For Trypho, the Hebrew Scriptures prove that Jesus could be neither Christ nor God; for Justin, those same Scriptures prove precisely the opposite!

The work as we have it (some of the original introduction is missing) opens with Trypho approaching Justin because of his philosopher's gown. Justin then gives his testimony, of how a 'certain old man' once engaged him in conversation, pulled apart the Platonism he was then devoted to, and told him of how, long before the philosophers, prophets who spoke by the Divine Spirit

---

6. It is sometimes suggested that Justin was unable to distinguish the Son from the Spirit properly. This is almost certainly unfair, and due partly to his willingness to speak of the eternal Word as 'a spirit', and partly to the fact that, for instance, he believed that the 'holy spirit' that descended on Mary in Luke 1:35 was the Word (*1 Apology* 33). Yet he never fails to differentiate between that 'spirit' and the Spirit.

announced the true God together with his Son. Then 'straightway a flame was kindled in my soul'.[7]

Trypho, hugely disappointed that Justin was not the sophisticated Greek philosopher he had taken him for, tells him that Christians are needlessly suffering for mere fabrications. He also adds that Christians cannot be righteous, because they do not follow the law (especially, they remain uncircumcised). Justin replies that Trypho has interpreted the law carnally (thinking that physical circumcision is of value), whereas he should understand it spiritually (by circumcising the heart). For, if physical circumcision were necessary, Adam would have been created circumcised; yet when declared good, he was uncircumcised. Enoch, Noah and the earliest patriarchs, when found pleasing to God, were not circumcised; nor was Abraham, when he was justified. And what of women, who cannot be circumcised?

Trypho's next complaint is that Jesus was a man cursed in his death by God, not the glorious Son of Man prophesied by Daniel. Justin's response is that Trypho has failed to recognize that Christ was prophesied to come twice, and that Trypho has done so because he misinterprets Scripture. Psalm 110, for instance, cannot be about Hezekiah, as Trypho asserts, for Hezekiah was not a priest for ever; not could Isaiah 7 be about Hezekiah; nor could Psalm 72 be about Solomon, for kings did not bow down to him, nor did he reign to the ends of the earth.

From the question of whether Jesus is the prophesied Christ, Trypho then moves the debate on to whether Jesus is Lord and God:

> you utter many blasphemies, in that you seek to persuade us that this crucified man was with Moses and Aaron, and spoke to them in the pillar of the cloud; then that he became man, was crucified, and ascended up to heaven, and comes again to earth, and ought to be worshipped.[8]

Justin is thus drawn in to look at the appearances of God in the Old Testament:

---

7. *Dialogue* 8.
8. Ibid. 38.

> Then I replied, 'Reverting to the Scriptures, I shall endeavour to
> persuade you, that He who is said to have appeared to Abraham, and to
> Jacob, and to Moses, and who is called God, is distinct from Him who
> made all things, – numerically, I mean, not [distinct] in will.'[9]

Starting with Genesis 18 – 19, he argues that God appeared to
Abraham along with two angels, yet from Genesis 19:24 (where the
Lord rained down sulphur 'from the LORD') it can be seen that he
is distinct from the Lord in the heavens. For there are a 'number of
persons associated with one another' who can be called Lord and
God (he also refers to Gen. 1:26; 3:22; Pss 45:6–7; 110:1).[10] Because of
this, the Lord and God who appeared to Abraham, and who is distinct
from the Lord and God in the heavens, can be called the Angel (or
'messenger') of the Lord (he also examines Gen. 31:11–13; 32:22–30
to see more of the Angel). Justin's point is that God the Father is
utterly transcendent and invisible in the heavens. However, he is made
known by his Logos or Angel, who appeared to make God known to
the patriarchs and prophets, and who took flesh for our salvation.

To support his case that Jesus was this Logos or Angel, Justin
explains that 'Jesus' is the name of God: God said (in Exod.
23:20–21) that his name would be in the one sent ahead of Israel to
lead them into the Promised Land. That one was 'Hoshea', whose
name was changed in Numbers 13:16 to 'Joshua', the Hebrew
form of 'Jesus'.[11] Jewish failure to notice this, Justin argues, only
betrays their wilful ignorance of the Scriptures, for while they carefully study why Abram's name was changed to Abraham, they do
not think why Hoshea's name was changed to Joshua.

> Then Trypho remarked, 'Be assured that all our nation waits for Christ;
> and we admit that all the Scriptures which you have quoted refer to Him.
> Moreover, I do also admit that the name of Jesus, by which the son of
> Nave (Nun) was called, has inclined me very strongly to adopt this view.
> But whether Christ should be so shamefully crucified, this we are in

---

9. Ibid. 56.

10. Ibid. 62.

11. Ibid. 75.

doubt about. For whosoever is crucified is said in the law to be accursed, so that I am exceedingly incredulous on this point.'[12]

To which Justin responds with how the cross is foreshadowed in the Old Testament in such places as Numbers 21 and Psalm 22.

What is so important to notice here is that Justin restricts himself to arguing from the Hebrew Scriptures alone, knowing that the books that make up what we now call the New Testament will carry no weight with Trypho. In this, Trypho and Justin are agreed: the case for Christianity can be made or broken by the Hebrew Scriptures. This can also be seen in Justin's answer to Trypho's next question. Trypho asks if it can be true that Christians believe in a resurrection of the dead; Justin's answer is emphatic: those 'who say there is no resurrection of the dead, and that their souls, when they die, are taken to heaven; do not imagine that they are Christians', but his proof-text for Trypho comes from Isaiah 65![13]

The rest of the dialogue is essentially dedicated to the question of the inclusion of the Gentiles, to which Trypho objects. Yet (referring to Gen. 9:27) Justin insists that since the days of Noah, the inclusion of the Gentiles has been prophesied. Furthermore, Christ, he argues, alluding to Genesis 32, is the true Israel, wrestling with God and being injured in the process, so that those who are his might have God's blessing:

As therefore from the one man Jacob, who was surnamed Israel, all your nation has been called Jacob and Israel; so we from Christ, who begat us unto God, like Jacob, and Israel, and Judah, and Joseph, and David, are called and are the true sons of God, and keep the commandments of Christ.[14]

Unlike later church fathers such as Origen and Augustine, Justin does not find much allegory in the Bible; instead, he finds the Old Testament full of types (Moses' bronze serpent being a 'prototype'

12. Ibid. 89.
13. Ibid. 80–81.
14. Ibid. 123.

of the cross; Joshua's circumcision of the Israelites being a type
of Jesus' circumcision of the hearts of his people).[15] Yet he does
see an allegory relevant to the issue of the Gentiles. Prompted by
Paul's allegory of Abraham's two wives, Hagar and Sarah, he sees
an allegory in Jacob's two wives: Jacob's first, short-sighted wife,
Leah (through whom came Judah) represents old, ethnic Israel; his
second, beloved wife, Rachel, represents the new Israel.[16]

Justin sums up his argument with an appeal to Trypho, that if
he had read his Scriptures properly, he would have trusted Christ
and known these things. This, for Justin, is the heart of the issue:
Christians have not read their meaning into the Hebrew Scriptures,
but have interpreted them correctly:

> if you knew, Trypho . . . who He is that is called at one time the Angel
> of great counsel, and a Man by Ezekiel, and like the Son of man by
> Daniel, and a Child by Isaiah, and Christ and God to be worshipped
> by David, and Christ and a Stone by many, and Wisdom by Solomon,
> and Joseph and Judah and a Star by Moses, and the East by Zechariah,
> and the Suffering One and Jacob and Israel by Isaiah again, and a Rod,
> and Flower, and Corner-Stone, and Son of God, you would not have
> blasphemed Him who has now come, and been born, and suffered, and
> ascended to heaven; who shall also come again, and then your twelve
> tribes shall mourn. For if you had understood what has been written by
> the prophets, you would not have denied that He was God, Son of the
> only, unbegotten, unutterable God.[17]

With a final call from Justin to trust in Christ and believe him
instead of the rabbis, Trypho leaves, apparently 'not far from the
kingdom of God'.

Justin martyred
About five years later, Justin, along with six friends, was brought
before the prefect of Rome for refusing to sacrifice to the gods.

---

15. Ibid. 114.
16. Ibid. 134.
17. Ibid. 126.

He confessed he was a Christian, and was summarily flogged and beheaded. Fellow Christians then carefully buried his remains, as had become customary for a people who believed passionately that the bodies of believers have a future beyond death.

Irenaeus of Lyons

Irenaeus once wrote:

> Thou wilt not expect from me, who am resident among the Keltae, and am accustomed for the most part to use a barbarous dialect, any display of rhetoric, which I have never learned, or any excellence of composition, which I have never practised, or any beauty and persuasiveness of style, to which I make no pretensions.[18]

As a result, Irenaeus has become a somewhat forgotten theologian, quickly dismissed as blundering and confused. Certainly, he is difficult to access, and hard-going theologians tend to incite the wrath of the critics. However, Emil Brunner's reassessment of Irenaeus has become increasingly standard:

> In spite of the fact that in the formal sense Irenaeus was not a systematic theologian, yet – like Luther – he was a systematic theologian of the first rank, indeed, the greatest systematic theologian: to perceive connections between truths, and to know which belongs to which. No other thinker was able to weld ideas together which others allowed to slip as he was able to do, not even Augustine or Athanasius.[19]

Who was Irenaeus, then?

He was born somewhere around AD 130 and grew up in Smyrna in Asia Minor, where the then bishop, Polycarp, became his mentor and passed on his memories of the apostle John and

---

18. *Against Heresies* 1.preface.3.
19. E. Brunner, *The Mediator: A Study of the Central Doctrine of the Christian Faith*, tr. O. Wyon (London: Lutterworth, 1934), p. 262.

others who had seen the Lord. It was to be extremely important to Irenaeus that he had such a direct link back to the apostles. It is possible that he went with Polycarp to Rome – at any rate, both visited Rome. There Irenaeus seems to have learned from men such as Justin (he clearly borrowed much from him), as well as seeing how endemic the problem of heresy was there. He then travelled to Gaul and settled where a church had been founded quite recently in the capital city of Lugdunum (Lyons).

Then in 177 he was sent back as the church's delegate to Eleutherus, then bishop of Rome, perhaps to discuss the problem of false teaching in Gaul. At any rate, while he was away, a ferociously violent wave of persecution swept through Lyons; many of Irenaeus' friends and fellow-believers were horrifically tortured and killed, including the old bishop, Pothinus. When Irenaeus returned, he was chosen to succeed Pothinus as bishop.

After that, the only thing we know of his life is his intervention in the Paschal controversy. Victor, Eleutherus' successor as bishop of Rome, had threatened to excommunicate the churches of Irenaeus' native Asia Minor for celebrating Pascha (later called Easter) on 14 Nisan, rather than the following Sunday, as they did in Rome. Irenaeus wrote irenically to Victor and the bishops of the Asian churches, urging them that on such secondary matters both parties should be free to celebrate according to their own tradition. It was an important little incident, for it showed that, despite all Irenaeus' emphasis on unity in the apostolic tradition, he did not countenance unconditional submission to the bishop of Rome, and could allow for different practices in the church.

Irenaeus wrote a number of works of theology; today, though, apart from a number of fragments from his writings, we have only two complete works of his: *Detection and Refutation of What Is Falsely Called 'Knowledge'*, usually known simply as *Against Heresies*, and his much shorter *Demonstration of the Apostolic Preaching*. In these works we see the first serious attempts to formulate Christian doctrine into a coherent structure. Irenaeus is thus a key architect of Christian thought. As such it is unsurprising that his influence spread so rapidly and so far (a fragment of *Against Heresies*, dating from when Irenaeus was still alive, has been found at Oxyrhynchus in Egypt, the other side of the known world from where he wrote the work).

We actually have no idea when or how Irenaeus died, though later tradition has it that he was martyred on 28 June 202.

Against Heresies

By the middle of the second century a collection of sects we now lump together and call Gnosticism had infected much of the church with various odd mutations of Oriental and Greek philosophies. One branch in particular seemed to be thriving: Valentinianism. Its leading light, Valentinus, once expected to become the next bishop of Rome, was an influential, gifted and persuasive theologian who managed to draw a number of disciples to his peculiar beliefs. Quite a number in the church in Lyons had been won over. Irenaeus saw this Gnosticism as a many-headed monster, threatening his flock. And, a pastor at heart, through his great five-volume work *Against Heresies* he set out to protect the Christians, convert the Gnostics from their error and bring them to saving knowledge and, ultimately, kill the monster. Certainly, *Against Heresies* struck Gnosticism a mortal blow.[20]

Book 1: The many-headed monster

Irenaeus begins with a description of the beast. According to Valentinianism, everything began with a collection of thirty angelic beings (known as 'aeons') who together made up the spiritual realm. Then one of the more junior aeons had a wicked thought. This wicked thought had to be removed from the perfect, spiritual realm, whereupon it became the basis for the physical cosmos. The logic of Genesis was thus reversed, with creation following a fall.

In so teaching, Gnosticism directly challenged the heart of the Christian gospel, for the creation, in such a model, was not

---

20. However, the fact that Gnosticism never quite died out is one reason why Irenaeus remains relevant today. Irenaeus believed that Valentinus had managed to come up with the definitive heresy that summed up and encapsulated all heresies. If there is any truth to that, it should be no surprise that we live today in a culture increasingly fed on a diet of rewarmed Gnosticism (witness the essential Gnostic themes of Dan Brown's *The Da Vinci Code* and Philip Pullman's *His Dark Materials* trilogy).

good but bad. The human body was thus a despicable tomb for
the valuable spirit and soul. And if that were the case, what of
the incarnation? For Gnosticism, the incarnation was impossible.
Instead, 'Christ passed through Mary just as water flows through
a tube' (in other words, without taking on real flesh).[21] As a result,
many Gnostics believed that Christ could not have died, but
instead that another was made to look like him and was crucified
in his place. Others believed that the cross was the moment when
the divine being, Christ, left the man, Jesus (hence Jesus' cry, 'My
God, my God why have you forsaken me?').

In any case, in Gnosticism there was not much need for Christ
to die, because the problem was not sin but having a body. Thus,
for the Gnostic, 'salvation' was not about having faith in Jesus,
but looking within to know the precious spark of the divine that
would one day be liberated from the body. This being the case,
Gnostic practice was always prone to lurch between two opposite
extremes. On the one hand, the radical split between the body and
the spirit allowed some Gnostics to indulge their flesh in the com-
forting knowledge that the spirit, like a pearl in the mud, would
remain entirely unspoiled. On the other hand, their hatred for the
body turned other Gnostics into radical ascetics, for although they
were of the world, they had no desire to be in it.

What was Jesus about, then? For Valentinus, all of Jesus' life
was a code, in which he symbolically acted out and so revealed
what had taken place within the spiritual realm. The thirty years
of his 'hidden life' before his public ministry spoke of the thirty
aeons; the apostasy of Judas, the 'twelfth apostle', spoke of the sin
of the twelfth aeon, and so on. That none of this was obvious was
precisely the point: Jesus, the Gnostics claimed, had not taught
openly, but in parables, only giving the secret knowledge of their
meaning to his most trusted disciples. This knowledge could not
be seen clearly in the apostolic writings acknowledged by the
church, but was passed on secretly by oral tradition. This all seems
very tendentious to us today, but given how highly oral tradition

---

21. *Against Heresies* 1.7.2; 3.11.3 (references to *Against Heresies* consist of three
    numbers, identifying the book, the chapter and the section, respectively).

was valued in the second century, this was a very serious threat to the church.

The Gnostics, then, were those who had this secret tradition of knowledge (the word 'Gnostic' comes from *gnōsis*, the Greek word for 'knowledge') and who sought not salvation in any normal sense, but the knowledge that within themselves lay a spiritual spark of the divine. It was this that Irenaeus sought to oppose in his *Detection and Refutation of What Is Falsely Called 'Knowledge'*.[22]

Book 2: Slaying the dragon

Irenaeus' first objection was that Gnosticism had denied that God is the Creator. For, it argued, the one who had organized a cosmos that by its very existence was evil must himself be evil. Yahweh, the Creator and God of Israel, could not then be the true and supreme God made known in the New Testament; he could only be a wicked angelic pretender to supreme deity. Some, like Marcion, thus sought to distance the God of Jesus as far as possible from Yahweh by rejecting the Hebrew Scriptures and any apostolic writings that connected them. Others, such as the Cainite sect, were more radical and sought to hold up Cain (and all the other characters of the Old Testament who refused to submit to Yahweh) as role models for their wise refusal to submit to the evil impostor-god.

For Irenaeus, their suggestion that there might be a God higher than the Father was precisely their downfall. Believing in such a multiplicity of competing gods, it was no wonder that Gnostic thought was so diverse and self-contradictory. In contrast, he holds up the unity of the church's faith, a unity that flows from the fact that one Father, by his one Word, in one Spirit, gives one truth to one church for all.

---

22. For centuries, without much other evidence left of what Gnosticism was like, people wondered how fair Irenaeus had been in his assessment of Gnosticism. Had he simply set up a straw man? Yet in 1945 a collection of Gnostic writings was found at Nag Hammadi in Egypt (the most famous being the so-called *Gospel of Thomas*), giving an unprecedented insight into Gnostic teachings. Judging by these, most scholars now agree that Irenaeus was remarkably accurate in his description of Gnosticism.

However, Irenaeus argues, the root of the problem lay in how the Gnostics read Scripture. He suggests that they treated Scripture like a mosaic, taking whichever tiles they liked and rearranging them to come up with whatever image they fancied, so transforming the original picture, of, say, a king, into something entirely different, perhaps that of a dog or fox. They are thus, he says, perverters, abusers and evil interpreters of the Scriptures. Yet how exactly they are so is vital for Irenaeus. The reason they warp Scripture is because they read it based on non-scriptural principles, forcing it to fit into an alien mould. Scripture cannot be so read, according to Irenaeus; rather, Scripture can only be understood by Scripture. No other knowledge, theological system or oral tradition can accurately mediate the true meaning of Scripture.[23]

Book 3: A grand plan
If Irenaeus were to respond properly, he could not limit himself to attacking the so-called 'knowledge' of the Gnostics; he had to present the true knowledge of which they were actually ignorant. From here on, then, Irenaeus sets out to show what a correct interpretation of Scripture looks like.

It all starts with the one God. First, the Father (the Creator) and the Son (the Saviour) are not two different gods but one; secondly, God is one in the sense that the God of the Old Testament is the God of the New Testament (for obvious reasons, Irenaeus, like Justin, seeks to make both points from the Old Testament, using especially Gen. 19:24 and Pss 45, 110 to show the Father and the Son at work together in the Old Testament).

From here he moves to demonstrate that the eternal Word truly became flesh, rather then merely resting on, or pretending to be, a

---

23. Cf. *Against Heresies* 3.12.9. This *sola Scriptura* principle at the heart of Irenaeus' theology gives the lie to the misconception that Irenaeus gave a higher authority to apostolic succession and tradition than he did to Scripture. He did value the direct connection between the apostles and their successors, the bishops, in his day; however, that never served as a grid to force Scripture through, but as proof that the plain truth of Scripture had been preserved and not distorted by the church.

real man called Jesus. Irenaeus saw that if God despised flesh and so refused to become incarnate, there would be no salvation. To deny the incarnation, as the Gnostics did, is thus spiritually murderous. It would also rob Christians of all loyalty to Christ in the face of martyrdom, for if Christ did not really suffer death on the cross, but flew off, leaving another in his place, why should Christians who seek to follow him suffer? Rather, Irenaeus argues, Christians must affirm that Jesus Christ is truly God with us who came in real flesh.

Why, though, would God take on flesh? To answer this, Irenaeus now articulates the theory for which he is most famed: 'recapitulation'. In a nutshell, Irenaeus' idea of recapitulation is that Christ is the second Adam, undoing the evils brought about by the first Adam. Sin and death had entered the world on a bad Friday (Irenaeus placed Gen. 3 in day six of creation), through a tree (the tree of knowledge), through one man eating, aided by a disobedient betrothed virgin (Eve); life and salvation came on Good Friday, through a tree (the cross), through one man fasting (in the desert), aided by an obedient betrothed virgin (Mary).[24]

However, the word 'recapitulation' can be a little misleading (as well as off-putting!), giving the impression that Irenaeus imagined Christ simply reversing the fall to take us back to Eden. Irenaeus was a long way from seeing salvation as a U-turn, though: for him, salvation was about going through death to a perfection never possible in Eden. Irenaeus believed that Adam and Eve were never God's goal; they were only children, and the project of salvation was about humanity being brought to maturity. This was achieved in Christ, who came as an infant and grew to full maturity for us.[25]

---

24. For Irenaeus, Mary was necessary to salvation in a similar way to how Joseph and Judas were necessary (though clearly she was more important, Jesus inheriting his humanity solely from her). However, the role Irenaeus gave Mary played a part in the rise of the theory that Mary is 'co-redemptrix' alongside Christ.

25. It was partly for this reason that Irenaeus believed that Christ's incarnate ministry lasted from the age of thirty to fifty (the career length of the Levitical priests), Jesus dying in his early fifties as (what was for the second century) a mature old man (*Against Heresies* 2.22).

Adam was a 'pattern of the one to come' (Rom. 5:14); an image of the true Image of God, Jesus Christ; filled with breath as a type of the one filled with the Spirit.

Humanity, from the moment of its creation, then, was destined for Spirit-filled maturity in Christ. Yet if Christ were to bring the humanity that was created to its goal, he could not 'pass through Mary as water through a tube', or take a body afresh from the earth as Adam had been; he needed an umbilical cord of continuity with the race of Adam. Only by taking the actual flesh of Adam's race (through Mary) could Adam's flesh be saved. In this way the humanity that had been created would be redeemed.

From this it looks like Irenaeus is moving towards saying that humanity was created *in order* to be saved, which raises some profound questions: Would Christ have come if Adam had not sinned? Did Adam fall, or was he pushed? Irenaeus puts it like this: just as God appointed a monster to swallow Jonah for a time, so he ordained Satan to swallow up humanity in death for a time. But humanity was subjected to death in hope, so that God might have mercy, and the apparent victory of Satan gave way to the true and final victory of Christ.[26] Death, then, was brought about as an act of judgment; but there was mercy in the judgment, for death prevented man from being immortal in his state of naked alienation from God. Through death humanity would be brought to be more than mere creatures, as they were created; through death man would become God.

At this point Irenaeus really does start to sound quite strange, and it is easy to leap to wrong conclusions. Yet Irenaeus is emphatic: man was created so that, ultimately, he might become God. Irenaeus is not suggesting that, somehow, we will one day transcend and shed our humanity. Far from it: just as when God became man he remained completely God, so when man becomes God he remains completely man. What Irenaeus means is that the hope of humankind is not merely that we might be declared 'not guilty', or even that we might know God from afar; the hope of humankind is to participate in the being of God, sharing in

---

26. Ibid. 3.20.1.

the Triune life of God as we are loved by the Father through the Son as adopted children in the eternal fellowship of the Spirit. God is glorified and man reaches his goal when man is brought to share God's life and glory. That, according to Irenaeus, is the grand plan of creation, that man might be included in the glory of God.

Book 4: One God, one Word, one plan
Of course, Irenaeus' whole description of God's grand plan depended on Marcion's being wrong, on the fact that it is the one same God who creates, reveals and redeems. It is this that Irenaeus now goes on to demonstrate. The one true God, he asserts, has only one great project because he only ever arranges anything through his Word, and with reference to him. That is, the Father always makes himself known and achieves his purposes through his Son, meaning that the Old and New Testaments have exactly the same purpose:

> the law never hindered them from believing in the Son of God; nay, but it even exhorted them so to do, saying that men can be saved in no other way from the old wound of the serpent than by believing in Him who, in the likeness of sinful flesh, is lifted up from the earth upon the tree of martyrdom, and draws all things to Himself, and vivifies the dead.[27]

Thus Old Testament believers did not worship a different God, but had the same faith as Christians, for through the Word they knew the Father, and through the Spirit foresaw the coming of the Son. In fact, Irenaeus often refers to the Word simply as 'the one who spoke with Moses', because he believed that the Word spoke with Moses and the other prophets and patriarchs to proclaim to them the salvation he would bring, and hence draw them to his Father.[28] Thus the content of the apostolic proclamation in Acts was new to Jewish audiences in one respect only: that the same Word that the patriarchs had known had now come in the flesh.

27. Ibid. 4.2.7.
28. Ibid. 4.5.2; 4.9.1; 4.10.1; 4.16.3–4.

For nothing else [but baptism] was wanting to him who had been already instructed by the prophets: he was not ignorant of God the Father, nor of the rules as to the [proper] manner of life, but was merely ignorant of the advent of the Son of God.[29]

It was a powerful affirmation against Marcion that the Old Testament is Christian Scripture. For Irenaeus there could be no fundamental difference between the Old and New Testaments: the Father is always known through the Son. Yet if that is so, what was the point of the incarnation? It is to that question that Irenaeus turns in the final book.

Book 5: The salvation of the flesh

In the first few lines of Book 5, Irenaeus sums up his understanding of the incarnation in the famous words 'our Lord Jesus Christ, did, through His transcendent love, become what we are, that He might bring us to be even what He is Himself'.[30] Incarnation, then, is nothing like a mere theophany in Irenaeus' mind. Incarnation is the salvation of the flesh that the Old Testament believers looked forward to. Irenaeus believed that Jesus Christ, the Word of God, is the true Image of God. Adam was created in his image. And, as Adam was filled with breath, so Jesus Christ is eternally filled with the Spirit, whom Irenaeus also calls the 'Wisdom of God' and the 'Likeness of God'.[31] What happened in the incarnation was that the Image of God took human flesh so that that flesh might at last be filled with the Spirit with which the Image had always been filled. Thus flesh is taken into the Image of God and filled with the Likeness of God: humanity then truly becomes *Homo sapiens*, filled with the *Sapientia* (Wisdom) of God. Incarnation is thus the essential key to God's grand plan of bringing the fleshly humanity he created to its goal.

The reason Irenaeus finishes his work on this topic is because

---

29. Ibid. 4.23.2.
30. Ibid. 5.preface.
31. The early post-apostolic church almost universally believed that the figure of Wisdom in Prov. 8 is the pre-incarnate Christ. Irenaeus believed instead that Wisdom is the Spirit.

Gnosticism denied that the flesh could be saved or have any hope beyond death. In stark contrast to Christianity, the Gnostic hope was for a resurrection of the spirit, not the flesh, such that, once the body had died, the spirit alone would live on in heaven. To make their point, the Valentinians in Lyons loved to quote 1 Corinthians 15:50 ('flesh and blood cannot inherit the kingdom of God'). For Irenaeus, this was to deny salvation itself. Instead, seeing that the resurrected Jesus had flesh (Luke 24:39), Irenaeus explained that the apostle Paul's argument moved in completely the opposite direction. Flesh on its own cannot inherit the kingdom of God; however, through the incarnation, the Spirit is joined to flesh so that the flesh might be saved. Whereas in Gnosticism, spirit and flesh must go their separate ways after the sweet release of death, Irenaeus saw salvation being about the marriage of flesh and Spirit. In the incarnation Christ joined the Spirit to human flesh so that human flesh might have a future. Thus the resurrection hope of a spiritual body is not to be less bodily, but to be more truly and completely so, the Spirit coming not to rob but to redeem man from all that impoverishes and undermines him, and bring him to the end for which his flesh was created.

Perhaps, above all, the Eucharist was Irenaeus' crowning proof of the salvation of the flesh: mere bread becomes more than what it once was. The bread is not replaced by something different (just so, the flesh is not replaced by the Spirit in the resurrection); yet the bread is more than mere bread. And, more simply, the Eucharist is all about physical things: bread, wine, body, blood. That being the case, Irenaeus simply could not see how Gnostics, who despised the physical, could take the material elements with any degree of consistency.

Irenaeus rounds off with another 'recapitulation' – as Christ gathers up and brings all human history to a head, so the Antichrist will gather up and bring all evil to a head. Then, as was common in the second century, Irenaeus expected the righteous would enjoy a thousand years of Sabbath rest before the wicked were resurrected to final judgment.

The Demonstration of the Apostolic Preaching
While for a long time it was known that Irenaeus had written a work called *The Demonstration of the Apostolic Preaching*, the work

itself had vanished long ago. Then, in 1904, a manuscript was discovered in a church library in Erevan in Armenia. Its publication (in 1907) was eagerly awaited, because this was the earliest Christian work written explicitly to summarize the faith.

Written shortly after *Against Heresies*, the *Demonstration* sets out to give one Marcianus a brief summary of Christian teaching so that he might 'understand all the members of the body of truth'. As the title suggests, it also seeks to demonstrate that the apostolic preaching is the true message of the Old Testament. Irenaeus starts off by giving the content of the apostles' message. It must begin, he says, with the one God, who is the Creator, his Word and Spirit; and from baptism on, the Father, Son and Spirit become the structure of our faith. He then swoops down, through an observation of the creation of the heavens, to how humanity was created to walk and talk with the Word of God in paradise, and how we fell. From there he races through the Old Testament to show how the incarnation and the inclusion of the Gentiles were foretold.

In the second half of the work Irenaeus aims to demonstrate that the whole content of the apostolic preaching comes from the Old Testament. First he shows that Jesus is the eternal Word of God, known by patriarchs and prophets; that he was in the beginning with the Father; that he appeared to Abraham and Jacob, and spoke to Moses from the bush. Next he explains how the fact that the eternal Word has now become God with us, in our flesh, born of a virgin, was also promised in the Old Testament. From virgin birth he moves to prophecies of the life, miracles, sufferings, crucifixion, resurrection and ascension of the incarnate Christ, as well as of the calling of the Gentiles (which was still an issue for dialogue with Jews).

Irenaeus concludes with a warning to avoid all heresies, of which, he says, there are three basic types: the first denies the Father and imagines another God; the second denies the Son and imagines there was no incarnation, and thus no love of God for humanity or our flesh; the third denies the Spirit and despises the true prophecy of Scripture. Instead of falling into such errors, Irenaeus bids the reader to hold to the oldest and truest preaching, that of the true God, the coming of his Son and the gift of his Spirit.

Going on with Justin and Irenaeus

Justin and Irenaeus are always in danger of being confined to the mental museum as mere historical curiosities, and yet the issues they deal with are all still vital: How should Scripture be interpreted? Who is God? What is salvation? However, reading them can be hard. Starting out with a theologian of the second century often feels like arriving on a different planet, for, unsurprisingly, the further one is removed in time from an author, the more alien he tends to feel. As a result, modern readers have to exercise special patience not to force second-century beliefs into more familiar patterns of thought that can be more rapidly digested or rejected.

Unfortunately, mountains of books and articles on these early theologians are guilty of exactly that, and so readers must be careful not to rely blithely on the secondary literature. The fact is, we do not have that much original material to work from, which means it is often quicker and easier to go straight to the horse's mouth.

Sadly for Justin, readers without languages or pots of cash have to rely on some rather rickety old nineteenth-century translations, but all his extant works are easily available online (at <http://www.ccel.org>) or in the *Ante-Nicene Fathers* series (vol. 1). His *Dialogue with Trypho* is probably the best place to start for an all-round feel of Justin's thought.

Irenaeus' *Against Heresies* is also available online (at <http://www.ccel.org>) and in the *Ante-Nicene Fathers* series in the same translation (also vol. 1). It is well worth a few hours' time, though a warning to the reader: unless you are very keen to learn about second-century Gnosticism, skip the first two books! For those who just want a taster of Irenaeus, John Behr's translation of *The Demonstration of the Apostolic Preaching* (Crestwood, N. Y.: SVS, 1997) is excellent, and comes with very helpful notes and introduction, highly recommended. For anyone interested in following up Irenaeus' main themes of incarnation and recapitulation, one outstanding introduction is worth mentioning: Gustaf Wingren, *Man and the Incarnation: A Study in the Biblical Theology of Irenaeus* (Edinburgh: Oliver & Boyd, 1959).

Justin Martyr and Irenaeus timeline

100?	Justin born
100–160?	Marcion
100–160?	Valentinus
130?	Irenaeus born
153–5	Justin's *First* and *Second Apologies*
155?	Martyrdom of Polycarp
160?	*Dialogue with Trypho*
160–225	Tertullian
165?	Justin martyred
175–89	*Against Heresies* and *The Demonstration of the Apostolic Preaching*
177	Persecution in Lugdunum (Lyons); Irenaeus sent to Rome, returns to become bishop
185–254	Origen
195?	Paschal controversy
202	Wave of persecution instigated by the emperor Septimius Severus. Irenaeus martyred?
303–12	The 'Great Persecution'
312	Conversion of the emperor Constantine to Christianity
325	Council of Nicea

3. AGAINST THE WORLD
Athanasius

Athanasius' name means 'immortal', and could hardly be more fitting. His life of high action and derring-do, his rapier-like mind, his ready smile and the sheer force of his personality all make him entirely unforgettable. Yet there is a greater reason why Athanasius deserves a place in any Christian hall of fame. As C. S. Lewis put it:

> His epitaph is *Athanasius contra mundum*, 'Athanasius against the world.' We are proud that our own country has more than once stood against the world. Athanasius did the same. He stood for the Trinitarian doctrine, 'whole and undefiled,' when it looked as if all the civilised world was slipping back from Christianity into the religion of Arius – into one of those 'sensible' synthetic religions which are so strongly recommended today and which, then as now, included among their devotees many highly cultivated clergymen. It is his glory that he did not move with the times; it is his reward that he now remains when those times, as all times do, have moved away.[1]

---

1. C. S. Lewis, Introduction to *On the Incarnation* by Athanasius (reprint, Crestwood, N. Y.: SVS, 1998), p. 9.

Athanasius' life

Athanasius was born somewhere around AD 296–8, and after that
we know virtually nothing certain about his youth or appearance.
Admirers said he had angelic good looks; opponents called him
a 'black dwarf' due to his diminutive stature, the one physical
trait we can be sure of. At quite a young age, though, he seems
to have been talent-spotted by Alexander, the bishop of the bus-
tling metropolis of Alexandria in Egypt, who provided him with a
first-rate theological education. During his early years, the young
Athanasius would also have seen, sweeping through the city, some
of the most intense waves of persecution that the Roman imperial authorities had ever mustered, killing off many of the most
prominent Christians of the generation above him.

Then in 318, Arius, a presbyter of the church in Alexandria,
began to accuse Alexander of failing to distinguish properly
between the Father, the Son and the Spirit.[2] Instead, Arius began
teaching that the Son was actually a created being, made by the
Father to go on and create the universe. A brilliant propagandist,
Arius put his theology into ditties, set them to well-known tunes,
and quickly whipped-up popular support for his views.[3] Mobs
were soon marching through the city chanting the slogans of Arius'
theology. Alexander responded by gathering just over a hundred
bishops to Alexandria to examine Arius' views. They quickly condemned the new teaching as heresy, removed Arius as a presbyter,
and forced him to leave the city. Far from putting a lid on the
problem, that just spread it: Arius fled to Nicomedia (near modern

---

2. Arius had received his theological training in Antioch, and so
   approached theology from a rather different angle to the theologians
   of Alexandria.

3. Singing their theology remained an effective Arian tactic for many
   years. Arian choirs used to sing through the night in the streets of
   Constantinople until the bishop, John Chrysostom, set against them
   choirs singing orthodox hymns (a showdown that, somewhat inevitably,
   ended up with the rival choirs in a street battle, after which the practice
   was made illegal for the Arians).

Istanbul), where the bishop, Eusebius, was supportive.[4] Eusebius used his powerful influence to help wage a campaign to win over any bishops who had not condemned Arius at Alexandria.

Not long after, Constantine, who had been a Christian and emperor of the western half of the Roman Empire for a little over a decade, added the eastern half to his domain. Perhaps because he saw Christianity as a potential force for unity, the next year (325) he invited bishops from across the empire – and some from without – to a general council at Nicea (also near modern Istanbul) to resolve the matter of Arius' teaching. Some three hundred came, including Alexander of Alexandria with his young secretary, Athanasius. How the bishops must have pinched themselves! But a few years earlier, the Roman Emperor had been the instigator of persecution, and some of the bishops themselves had been mutilated and scarred in the days of trial. Yet here they were, discussing theology in front of the emperor and being feasted by him!

The small Arian contingent fared badly, though: when they expressed their view of the Son of God they simply horrified the other bishops, some of whom covered their ears while others lost control and started a scuffle. The outcome of the council was the Nicene Creed, which contained the core anti-Arian affirmation that the Son was 'begotten, not made, of the same being of the Father' (*homoousion tō Patri*).[5] They would be words to which the young secretary, Athanasius, would devote his life as he defended them and drew from them the most profound theology.

Three years later Alexander died, and despite his youth Athanasius was appointed bishop of Alexandria. It was not long before the fickle emperor ordered him to reinstate Arius as a presbyter. Athanasius refused, unless Arius would sign the Nicene Creed. And so the troubles began. His opponents saw an opportunity and began circulating dark rumours: Athanasius had bought

---

4. Eusebius of Nicomedia should not be confused with his contemporary Eusebius of Caesarea, the great church historian.

5. The Greek word *homoousios* comes from *homo*, meaning 'same', and *ousia*, meaning 'being'.

the bishopric, had murdered and dismembered another bishop called Arsenius, and was using his severed hand for black magic. There was even a 'hand of Arsenius' doing the rounds to prove the point. Athanasius was summoned to a council at Tyre to answer for himself, and the hand was produced as evidence.

What had actually happened was that Arsenius had gone into hiding to get Athanasius convicted; however, he was tracked down, seized and spirited to Tyre. Then Athanasius had him brought in, wrapped in a cloak. Turning up the cloak he revealed one hand intact, paused dramatically, and then revealed the other hand intact before asking whence the third hand had been cut. Astonishingly, the council was so packed with Arians that Athanasius was still found guilty; and so he fled to Constantinople to appeal to the emperor. However, Athanasius was now such a figure of division that Constantine had little choice but to exile him to his imperial residence in Gaul (Treveri, now Trier, just to the west of Luxembourg). In Alexandria they rioted in protest.

While Athanasius was in exile, Arius died (though his cause was only growing) and Athanasius used the opportunity to warn the western half of the empire about the evils of Arianism. It was perhaps at this time that he also wrote his great double-barrelled work *Against the Heathen* and *On the Incarnation*.

Then, in 337, Constantine died and Athanasius was permitted to return to Alexandria, where he was met by cheering crowds. Yet within just two years new charges of irregularity were brought against him by the Arians and the situation in Alexandria became so dangerous that Athanasius was forced to leave for Rome. This time he had seven years in exile before he could return. When he did, it was to a golden decade of unhampered ministry.

But it was not the end of his troubles. Constantine's son, Constantius, the new emperor, was an Arian, and determined to root out all that Nicea had accomplished. That meant silencing Athanasius, who had become the figurehead of the orthodox Nicene party against the Arians. And so, in 356, five thousand Roman soldiers launched a surprise attack on the church where Athanasius was leading a vigil: the doors were burst open and the soldiers rushed in, swords drawn and arrows flying into the congregation. Athanasius ordered the people to leave so that nobody else might get hurt. However, in the mêlée his monks just grabbed him and smuggled him out through the confusion. A price was put on his head, and even the desert was scoured; but Athanasius was kept concealed by an army of loyal monks who simply moved him on when any imperial search party got too close. Sometimes he was hidden in a dry cistern, sometimes a cemetery – he even managed to go back and live under cover in Alexandria itself for a while. Yet Constantius' attack on the church, an attack meant to decapitate the Nicene party, only rebounded on him, for Athanasius used his exile to fashion the weapons that would bury Arianism, in particular his masterpiece *Against the Arians*. All in all, it was an astoundingly productive time in the desert: not only did he fire a deadly volley against the Arians; he also managed to produce a masterful defence of the Holy Spirit's deity in his letters to Serapion and, inspired by the desert monks, wrote his *Life of Antony*, a work that would be the fertilizer for the monastic movement.

After a few years Constantius died and was succeeded by Julian, the first (and last) pagan emperor since Constantine. Seeing Athanasius as a controversial catalyst for Christian disunity, he allowed him to return to his bishopric. Immediately, Athanasius had to face a new theology that had come on the scene while he was in hiding. It argued that the Nicene Creed's affirmation that the Son is 'of the *same* being (**homoousios**) of the Father' led rather too easily to a belief that the Father and the Son are not really distinguishable at all, but are, simply, the same. Instead, it was suggested, it would be better to speak of the Son as 'of a *similar* being (**homoiousios**) to the Father'.[6]

Athanasius summoned a council to meet in Alexandria, where he rejected both the idea that the Father and the Son are not really distinguishable, and the word *homoiousios*. Instead, he argued, the

---

6. Unhelpfully and unfairly, this position came to be called 'semi-Arianism' because of how it gave room to the Arian tendency to make the Son a different sort of being to the Father. However, it originated as an attempt to make clear that the Father and the Son are not to be thought of as mere masks or modes of a single being, but are distinct and distinguishable.

word *homoousios* does guarantee a distinction between the Father
and the Son, for it makes clear that there are two that must be
compared; on the other hand, it keeps shut the door that the word
homoiousios would open to the Arians.

At this point, readers may feel that Athanasius had, like a fussy
grammar teacher, got rather too hung up on trivial differences
between words. As Edward Gibbon put it, 'the difference between
the *Homoousion* and the *Homoiousion* is almost invisible to the nicest
theological eye'.[7] Yet, when at the Council of Alexandria the issue
was raised whether we should speak of the one *hypostasis* or the
one *ousia* of God, Athanasius argued that what mattered was not
the words themselves, but their meaning. In so doing, Athanasius
showed that he was no theologically trigger-happy scrapper, but a
sensitive and realistic pastor. He opposed the word *homoiousios*, not
because of the 'i' in the middle, but because it allowed the Son to
be seen as something less than truly God, a being merely 'similar'
to God.

It took only eight months for the emperor Julian, fearing
Athanasius' influence, to exile him once more. Athanasius headed
up the Nile to rejoin the desert monks, but even then retained his
usual sparkle: finding that he was being tracked, he turned the boat
around and soon came alongside that of the pursuers. Asked if he
had seen Athanasius, he replied with a twinkle in his eye, 'He is not
far off,' before drifting back down the river to steal into Alexandria
while the pursuers went on.

Briefly restored by the next emperor, he was, with a certain
degree of predictability, ordered to be seized in a night raid by
another, just the next year (365). Warned in time, Athanasius
fled into his fifth and last period of exile. By this time, however,
Athanasius was so influential that Egypt simply was not stable
with him in exile. And so he was recalled to live out his final years
as bishop. So popular had he become that when an anti-Nicene
bishop arrived in Alexandria in these years, he needed a mili-
tary escort for fear of attack. Many had hated Athanasius for his
extraordinary tenacity in defending the real deity of the Son and

---

7. E. Gibbon, *The Decline and Fall of the Roman Empire*, ch. 21, n. 155.

the Spirit, but the majority in Alexandria made it clear that precisely what many hated, they themselves loved. Athanasius died in 373, revered, but also victorious: his theology had triumphed over Arianism and would be canonized eight years later at the Council of Constantinople.

Against the Heathen *and* On the Incarnation

What was this triumphant theology? It is probably best captured by focusing our attention on Athanasius' main works: *Against the Heathen, On the Incarnation, Against the Arians* and *Life of Antony*.

Against the Heathen and *On the Incarnation* are really the titles of the two volumes of a single work. We do not know when it was written, but today it is thought to have been written around 335–6. Its agendum, though, is quite clear: it was written for a recent convert called Macarius as a basic introduction to the faith. From the start, then, this is pastorally concerned theology.

Against the Heathen

The first volume is a piercing theological critique of paganism and idolatry, focused on creation and the nature of sin and evil.

Athanasius starts with Jesus Christ, the Image of God the Father. Only by starting there, Athanasius suggests, can the true nature and purpose of creation be understood aright. Underpinning what it means for Christ to be the Image of the Father, he says, is the fact that Christ perfectly knows and enjoys communion with his Father (only thus can he truly 'image' him to the world). Humanity is then created in the image of Christ. The idea of 'image' having already been shown to be built upon personal knowledge and fellowship, this means that at the heart of human identity is the purpose to know and enjoy communion with Christ, in whose image we are made; and since he is the Image of the Father, through him we know the Father. That knowledge and communion is eternal life.

However, having been created with that purpose, humanity 'fell into lust of themselves, preferring what was their own to the contemplation of what belonged to God'.[8] Made to know and

_____

8. *Against the Heathen* 3.2.

contemplate God, they turned away, turning in to contemplate only themselves. But in so doing, humankind became addicted to the self and its bodily pleasures, an addiction that instantly flooded them with the fear of having those pleasures ripped away by death. Instead of knowing Christ the Word and Image of God, humanity now knew anxiety and despair. In that state they imagined other gods, but the only gods they could imagine were anxiety- and despair-inducing gods.

With this, Athanasius provides a glaringly different account of the origin of evil to those given by non-Christian alternatives, especially that of Greek philosophy. In pagan Greek thought, evil exists because matter exists, for matter is inherently imperfect. In Athanasius' scheme, evil arises out of a perverse use of human freedom. Evil comes from sin. As for what sin is, Athanasius argues that it is, at root, a relational problem, a turning away from God. But since God is the ground of all being, to turn away from God is to turn into nothingness. To walk into sin is to walk into unbeing. Sin is anti-being, which is why it never delivers the happiness it promises, for it is the very opposite of being. As for the gods manufactured by the sinful imagination, they too are anti-being and so corrosive of all that humanity was created to be.

From Christ as the Image of God, Athanasius then shifts to focus on Christ as the Word (*Logos*) of God, first, in relation to the soul. The soul, designed to know the *Logos*, is created logical. However, by turning away from the *Logos*, humankind has become illogical. The consequences are ugly, for just as the *Logos* controls the world, so we were given logic to control our bodies; but by abandoning that logic we allow our bodies to rule us, rather than vice versa. Thus the created order is inverted, meaning that the beauty, order and peace of knowing the *Logos* are exchanged for an imprisoning self-obsession that only delivers ugly disorder and fear.

Yet there is good news still to be found in the *Logos* of God. First, this is because of the Word's relation to creation. Creation, Athanasius says, was not only brought into being through the Word, but also, it continues to exist only as it is sustained each moment by the Word. Creation has no inherent ability to maintain itself in existence, but would simply cease to be without the Word.

By this Athanasius wants to show two things: (1) that the Word of God is not a creature, but the one on whom all creaturely being depends; and (2) that the Word is not distant from creation, but intimately related to it, sustaining its every moment.

That starts to look significant when Athanasius goes on to explain the Word's relation to the Father. That is, while the Word is distinct from the Father, he is so intimately related to him that he can be the Father's true 'Interpreter' and 'Angel' (or 'Messenger'). The result is that, while the Father is the Creator, there is no infinite abyss between him and creation as in Greek thought. Rather, he is intimately related to the Word, and the Word is intimately related to creation. If the Word were some third party called into being to bridge a gap between the Father and the creation, then of course the Father would remain infinitely distant from us and ultimately unknowable. However, because of his relation to the Word and the Word's relation to creation, the Father is 'not far from each one of us' (Acts 17:27).

Athanasius is making a bold claim about God's revelation of himself. It is that, because of the Word, there is no darkness or hidden aloofness in God, but an unrestrained self-giving. In the Word, God himself comes to us so that we may contemplate again the very being of God. To see and encounter the Word is to see and encounter God. It was precisely this good news that Arius had stolen away by denying the Word's relation to the Father. For Arius, there could be no true revelation of God; all the Word could reveal could only be a pale imitation of what God is really like. But, sighs Athanasius, to turn away from and deny the Word who reveals the Father to us is the very essence of the tragedy of sin. It is for just that reason that the Image of God, in whose image we were made, must come and remake humankind in his image and so remake fellowship with God.

On the Incarnation
In this second volume Athanasius moves from looking at the Word as *creator* to looking at the Word as *redeemer*; yet while the focus has shifted from creation to the redemption of creation, the subject is the same: the Word of God. The two volumes are emphatically about Jesus Christ, and understanding that helps to

make clear the central assertion of the second volume, that '*the renewal of creation has been wrought by the Self-same Word Who made it in the beginning*'.[9] However, the feel of *On the Incarnation* is quite different to that of *Against the Heathen*: here the dark themes of sin, evil and idolatry are driven out by the Word's redemption, making *On the Incarnation* (as C. S. Lewis put it) 'a sappy and golden book, full of buoyancy and confidence'.[10] And it is important to feel that difference (important, though not hard: Athanasius' punchy rhetoric is stirring stuff), for *On the Incarnation* is characterized by the idea of a happy, surprising overturning. Even the revelation of God through the Word is utterly surprising: 'The things which they, as men, rule out as impossible, He plainly shows to be possible . . . and things which these wiseacres laugh at as "human" He by His inherent might declares divine.'[11]

Athanasius starts with the creation of Adam and Eve, explaining that they were created good, but corruptible. Of course, they were then corrupted (one almost senses Athanasius suggesting that that was inevitably going to happen, for God's great purpose was to unite humankind to his own incorruptibility, so giving them incorruptible life). Once they were corrupted, though, what was God to do? Athanasius is adamant that it would not be worthy of God's goodness to allow humanity to be utterly destroyed. Yet destruction was exactly what was happening to humanity, for while the Word had called non-being into being in creation, through sin humankind was slipping back into non-being. What was needed was for the Word to come and recreate humanity.

It was not an entirely different humanity the Word was going to create from nothing, though. That would be no rescue; that would not resolve the problem of humanity's slide into darkness. Rather, he took on *our* humanity, and he took it from a virgin, so as not to inherit the taint of corruption. His was to be a pure humanity, not one that would itself die naturally.

Vitally, the only one who could come and recreate humanity

9. *On the Incarnation* §1, p. 26; italics original to translation.
10. Lewis, Introduction to *On the Incarnation*, p. 9.
11. *On the Incarnation* §1, p. 25.

was the Word and Image of God. First, because humanity was originally created in his image. Athanasius illustrates the point by comparing humanity made in the image of God to a portrait that has been defaced; rather than throwing it away, the subject of the portrait comes and sits again, so that his likeness can be redrawn. Humanity, then, can only be truly renewed by the self-same Image according to whom humanity was created. Secondly, Athanasius has already explained that being created in the image of God means being designed for personal knowledge of God, and this is something that only the Word of God can bring. The knowledge of God that the Word of God brings is precisely what humanity turned away from in sin as they turned inward and so turned into non-being. But when the Word of God restores knowledge of God, he saves humankind from corruption and non-being, from all 'this dehumanising of mankind'.[12] Only the Word and Image of God could rehumanize us.

Next comes the cross, 'the very centre of our faith': 'Death there had to be, and death for all, so that the due of all might be paid.'[13] Christ could not die just any death, though. First, he had to be executed. There was no cause for death within his spotless self, and so he would not have died had death not come from without, from the sin-filled world. Secondly, he had to be executed on a tree so as to become a curse for us (Gal. 3:13), and with his arms outstretched to draw and summon all men to himself. Thirdly, he had to be lifted up in the air, for 'the air is the sphere of the devil' (Eph. 2:2), and 'the Lord came to overthrow the devil and purify the air'.[14] Clearly, the killing of corruption in man (the root of all evil) would mean not only triumph over the devil, but also the healing and purification of the cosmos itself.

Then, on the third day, when his body should have corrupted, Christ was raised in victory over all corruption. In that moment, for the first time humanity enjoyed the incorruptibility beyond all death that God had planned for it. And we can be sure that Christ

---

12. Ibid. §13, p. 40.
13. Ibid. §19, p. 48; §20, p. 49.
14. Ibid. §25, p. 55.

is truly alive and victor over death, Athanasius argues, because only a living Christ could topple the old gods of paganism as he seemed to be doing all around, and only a living Christ could daily keep drawing so many to faith in himself. (This was clearly an apologetic that worked best in the years after the emperor Constantine had converted to Christianity.) Athanasius' other proof that Christ has conquered death is equally revealing of the age: it is that Christians, like children who make fun of a dead lion, 'despise death' and 'mock at it now as a dead thing robbed of all strength'.[15] Evidently, Athanasius had witnessed extraordinary courage in Christians facing martyrdom.

From there, he goes on to arguments that seek to persuade unbelieving Jews and Gentiles. First, the Jews: Athanasius rattles through the Old Testament to show how clearly it prophesied the coming of Christ, even including Daniel 9:24–25 to show that it is vain still to wait for the Christ to come, for Daniel specified when he would come, which is why no more prophets, priests or kings appeared in Israel after Jesus' day. Then he turns to the Gentiles, by which he means the Greeks, who thought it foolish to imagine that the Word could ever become flesh. Athanasius rejects their sneer as mere inconsistency, for, he says, they acknowledge a Word or *Logos* of God who is united to the cosmos as a whole (and even speak of the cosmos as the 'body' of the Word); yet if the Word can be united to all the cosmos, why is it foolish to say that he has united himself to a part of it? And Christ, he says, is the Word of God, not a mere man: how else, Athanasius asks, could he have defeated the gods? Nor is he a mere magician: he has destroyed magic. Nor is he a demon, for he drives out demons.

Some of the apologetic arguments near the end of the work strike us today as less than convincing, even if they are revealing of the times. But when he finally returns to the main argument, he becomes magisterial again. That is: why the incarnation? 'He, indeed, assumed humanity that we might become God.'[16] Clearly, Athanasius is not speaking of our becoming God in the sense of

---

15. Ibid. §27, p. 57.
16. Ibid. §54, p. 93.

leaving our humanity behind. That would conflict with everything he has argued for about the recreation of humanity. Rather, he is speaking of being brought into the intimate communion of God, knowing the Father just as Christ knows the Father.

Just as Athanasius made a bold claim about God's revelation, this now is a bold claim about God's salvation. Salvation, according to Athanasius, is not about being given a 'saved' status or a catalogue of blessings by a distant God; it is about entering the very communion of the Father and the Son. And again, this was precisely what Arius had taken away: by making the Son a mere creature, however exalted, he had denied the Son's real communion with the Father. In Arius' mind, then, the Son would be entirely unable to bestow communion with the Father, for the Son never knew it himself. Thus for Arius there could be no true communion with God.

Two criticisms are commonly levelled at Athanasius' theology, especially that of *On the Incarnation*: that he has left out the Spirit, and that he never allows the Word to become fully and truly human.

First, the absence of the Spirit. It is quite true that in these earlier works, Athanasius did not give much space to the Spirit (in that, while he repeatedly mentions the Spirit as one of the divine Three, he never unpacks the Spirit's role). It is entirely understandable, given that Arius' denial of the Son's deity was the pressing concern of the time, yet one misses the added richness that might have been there. That said, it would be entirely unfair to say that this was an ongoing problem in Athanasius' theology. During Athanasius' third exile, his good friend and fellow bishop Serapion wrote to ask for his advice on how to respond to those who denied the deity of the Spirit. Athanasius replied with four letters arguing that the Spirit is *homoousios* with the Father and the Son; indeed, if the Spirit is the one who comes to us to knit us into the Godhead, he must be God.

As for his Christology, the charge is that Athanasius imagines the Word not truly becoming human, but wearing his humanity like a detachable outer skin or, in modern terms, a kind of space-suit. For many years this has been the accepted line on Athanasius, and is based on how, a number of times, Athanasius refers to Jesus' body as the 'instrument' the Word 'uses'. Connected to this is the suggestion that Athanasius was so ensnared by a philosophical notion of God's absolute immutability that he could never imagine God 'becoming' anything, let alone flesh. Thus, the line goes, the Word kept himself safely detached from the spacesuit of his humanity and thus preserved his completely unchanging nature.

The argument, however, has been efficiently shredded in recent years.[17] First, the idea that Athanasius' Christology was driven by such a philosophy of God's immutability is an argument from silence. Instead, it seems that what Athanasius meant is that, when the Word became man, he still remained himself; he had not metamorphosed from being the Word into something entirely different (a man). He was still the Word, but now *also* a man. As for his language of the Word using his humanity as an 'instrument', what was meant was not that his humanity was like an external object he could pick up and put down at will; it is quite simply that his humanity was the means by which he saved humanity. 'He, indeed, assumed humanity that we might become God.' In fact, in some less-studied letters of his, Athanasius is as explicit as he could be that Christ's humanity was no husk, but complete.[18] It had to be, he argued, if Christ was ever to heal humanity completely.

Against the Arians
It was during his third exile, in the desert, on the run from the emperor's search parties, that Athanasius wrote this, the work that would ensure the immortality of his name more than anything else he did. It would do so since his discourses *Against the Arians* turned out to be *the* seminal defence of the Son's eternal deity and the stake through the heart of Arius' theology.

Discourse 1
The opening words show how seriously Athanasius took the Arian threat: 'Of all other heresies which have departed from the truth it

---

17. This is largely the work of Khaled Anatolios, whose arguments are summarized in his superb *Athanasius: The Coherence of his Thought* (New York: Routledge, 1998), pp. 70–72.
18. *Letter to the People of Antioch* 7; Letter 59.7.

is acknowledged that they have but devised a madness . . . whereas one heresy, and that the last . . . has now risen as harbinger of Antichrist, the Arian.' There would be no amicable agreement to disagree here!

First, Athanasius sets up his target by explaining what Arianism is. Arius had started with a philosophical presupposition of what God must be like: God by nature was 'ungenerated' or uncaused; in fact, he held, 'ungenerate' served as about the most basic definition of God. It follows, then, that since the Son is begotten or generated by the Father, he cannot truly be God. Rather, being begotten, he must have an origin: he must have come into being at some point and must therefore be a creature. Thus the eternal Son disappeared in a puff of philosophy – unsurprisingly, for Arianism was rationalist monotheism incarnate, 'one of those "sensible" synthetic religions which are so strongly recommended today and which, then as now, included among their devotees many highly cultivated clergymen' (as C. S. Lewis put it).

According to Arius, then, the Son of God is utterly unlike God; exalted, perhaps, but a mere creature, made so that he might make a creation that the Father was always too transcendent to have anything to do with. As such, it is not that we were created for the Son; rather, the Son was created for us and allowed to participate in certain divine characteristics as a gift. Thus, while he can be spoken of as 'God', he is not actually God, nor does he really know God, but is 'God' to us.

Athanasius' first response is to attack the methodology of the Arians (or 'Ario-maniacs' as he preferred to call them). Essentially, he argues, they get their notion of God from speculation: human sons, they said, start existing at some particular point, when they are begotten; so it must be with the Son of God. 'When they thus speak,' replied Athanasius, 'they should have inquired of an architect, whether he can build without materials; and if he cannot, whether it follows that God could not make the universe without materials.'[19] It is simply not possible, he argued, to work upwards like that towards a real knowledge of God.

---

19. *Against the Arians* 1.23.

Rather, 'it is more pious and more accurate to signify God from the Son and call Him Father, than to name Him from His works only and call Him Unoriginate'.[20] That is, Christians pray to the Father, not to 'the Unoriginate', for Father he is, not merely some abstractly defined 'Unoriginate' being. And it is only possible to know God as Father 'from the Son'. However, if we first define God by something such as being the Creator, we will define God abstractly (as something like 'Unoriginate' or 'ungenerate') and so define the Son out of his deity. And when we do that, we find ourselves worshipping a God who is not a real Father and who does not really have a Son. We have become idolaters. This, Athanasius holds, is the essential Arian problem: by trying to know God other than through the Son, they had come to know an entirely different God. And this was why Athanasius held the deity of the Son to be non-negotiable, for it is only by knowing the Son that any can ever know the God who is.

That said, while the Arians had not got their understanding of God from Scripture, they would use Scripture to support their view. In particular, they liked Hebrews 1, with verses such as 'You are my Son, today I have begotten you' (v. 5) and its references to the exaltation of the Son (an exaltation that seemed to them incompatible with the Son being truly God). Athanasius, citing the Hebrews 1 references to the Son as God on his eternal throne (from Ps. 45) and the Son as creator (from Ps. 102), counters that the Son was always worshipped as Lord in the Old Testament. As for the exaltation/begetting language, Athanasius explains that the Son took on humanity, and that was what was then exalted in Christ's ascension: united to the Son, the humanity was now exalted to the filial status that the Son had always enjoyed. Indeed, that adoption was the purpose of the incarnation.

Discourse 2

In the first discourse, Athanasius had already noted in passing that Arius' God, for all his transcendence, was actually weak and needy, unable to achieve what he wanted without his created helper, the

---

20. Ibid. 1.34.

Son; he was a God 'in process of completion as time goes on'.[21]
Now Athanasius provides the orthodox alternative: God, he says,
must be Father before he could ever be a creator. That is, in order
to be capable of going out in creation, he must be fruitful and
life-giving by nature: such the Father is (being *Father*); such Arius'
lonely 'Unoriginate' was not.

Athanasius thus revealed that his God was an utterly different
being to the God of the Greek philosophy of his day. His God was
not static, but a dynamic, personal being, inherently outgoing and
productive. Athanasius compares the Father to a fountain and a
sun: just as a fountain must pour forth water to be a fountain, and
just as a sun must have a radiance, so the Father must 'pour forth',
'radiate' or beget the Son in order to be who he is, the Father. In
contrast, Arius' talk of a Father without a Son signified a barren
God who was like a dry fountain or a sun that does not shine.

Much of the rest of the second discourse is then taken up
with proving from the Old Testament (and thus from before the
incarnation) that Christ

> is Lord and King everlasting, seeing that Abraham worships Him as
> Lord, and Moses says, 'Then the Lord rained upon Sodom and upon
> Gomorrah brimstone and fire from the Lord out of heaven;' and David
> in the Psalms, 'The Lord said unto my Lord, Sit Thou on My right
> hand;' and, 'Thy Throne, O God, is for ever and ever; a sceptre of
> righteousness is the sceptre of Thy Kingdom;' and, 'Thy Kingdom is an
> everlasting Kingdom;' it is plain that even before He became man, He
> was King and Lord everlasting, being Image and Word of the Father.[22]

In fact, more than any other, it was an Old Testament text,
Proverbs 8:22, that lay at the heart of the exegetical battles
Athanasius had with the Arians, and large swathes of *Against the
Arians* are given over to issues surrounding it. All sides agreed
that Wisdom was a name for Christ, but, unlike the Hebrew text,
the Septuagint (on which both sides relied) had Wisdom being

---

21. Ibid. 1.17.
22. Ibid. 2.13.

'created' in Proverbs 8:22. Athanasius simply treated this as he had
treated Hebrews 1, by stating that the 'creation' referred to Christ's
humanity, 'created' for him at the incarnation.

This leads Athanasius into an extended discussion of what it
means for Christ's humanity to be founded 'before the world'.
Athanasius understands that even before creation the Father had
his purpose to save through Christ, and this understanding he
develops into what is almost certainly the most detailed doctrine
of election before Augustine's. It is rather different to Augustine's
belief, though, which tended to focus (especially in later years) on
individuals being predestined to adoption; instead, Athanasius
holds that the Son was the predestined one, and that only in him
are we chosen:

> How then has He chosen us, before we came into existence, but that,
> as he says himself, in Him we were represented beforehand? and how
> at all, before men were created, did He predestinate us unto adoption,
> but that the Son Himself was 'founded before the world,' taking on Him
> that economy which was for our sake? . . . and how did we receive it
> 'before the world was,' when we were not yet in being, but afterwards
> in time, but that in Christ was stored the grace which has reached us?
> Wherefore also in the Judgment, when every one shall receive according
> to his conduct, He says, 'Come, ye blessed of My Father, inherit the
> kingdom prepared for you from the foundation of the world.' How then,
> or in whom, was it prepared before we came to be, save in the Lord who
> 'before the world' was founded for this purpose.[23]

Discourse 3
Athanasius still did not feel that he had made the relationship
between the Father and the Son sufficiently clear, and this he now
proceeds to do, with the Nicene formula (that the Son is 'begotten,
not made, of the same being of the Father' [*homoousion tō Patri*])
clearly at the forefront of his mind.[24]

---

23. Ibid. 2.76.

24. The Arians' first objection to the word *homoousios* was that it was
    unscriptural. Yet, as Athanasius effectively demonstrated, not only

Nicea had clarified a distinction between being 'begotten' and being 'made' that had not been sufficiently obvious beforehand, but which would be crucial for Athanasius' doctrine of God (as well as for the church as a whole). That is, a subject can 'beget' only the *same* kind of being as itself; thus men 'beget' men and the Father 'begets' the Son. On the other hand, a subject can only 'make' a *different* kind of being; thus men 'make' doughnuts and God 'makes' the world. Men cannot 'beget' doughnuts, nor God 'beget' the world; just so, men cannot 'make' men, nor God 'make' the Son.

What Nicea had not made clear was what the word 'being' (*ousia*) meant, and it was because of this that some felt the word *homoousios* unhelpfully suggested a lack of distinction between the Father and the Son. Athanasius' whole approach makes it quite apparent, though, that such fears were unfounded. *Homoousios* does not mean that the Father and the Son consist of the same generic material (*ousia*) in the way that two sweets come from the same butterscotch. That would unacceptably imply two Gods. Rather, the Father and the Son are *homoousios* in the sense that they are the same being, the same God.

Athanasius makes clear what he sees as the implication of the Nicene formula by putting the emphasis on the Son's 'same being of the Father' (*homoousion **tō Patri***). It is not, then, that there is some third thing, a divine material or 'being' (*ousia*), that the Father and Son share. The Son is not said to be from the being of *God*. The Son is *of the Father*. This means that there is no God-stuff underlying the Father or the Son. The Father's being is not anything more fundamental than that he is the Father. He did not will to become the Father at some point so that we might ask what he was before that and so what he was more fundamentally. Rather, God is the Father begetting the Son, and that begetting is not an add-on to who God is.

---

was the whole Arian approach fundamentally non-scriptural but they themselves also used unscriptural terms – referring to God as 'Ungenerate' and insisting on such phrases as 'there was a time when the Son was not'. The reality was, terms from outside the Bible had to be used to counter the Arian tendency to twist all scriptural terms to fit its non-scriptural philosophical framework.

The Nicene Creed began with the words 'We believe in one God, the Father'. It had not spoken of the 'Ungenerate' but of the 'Father'. What Athanasius sought to establish was that if 'Father' is a real statement about this God's very being, then he cannot have become Father at some point. The Father must have his being begetting the Son. That means that 'when we call God Father, at once with the Father we signify the Son's existence'.[25] Or, to put it another way, if the Father really is eternally Father this means that the Son must be eternal.

And this, Athanasius is able to conclude, becomes the problem for the Arians, for by denying the eternal Son, they had denied the Father's very being and identity and could have no part in him. It is a conclusion that reveals why Athanasius was so unswerving: he saw that he was fighting for the very identity of God, the knowledge of whom is salvation. And if the Arians did not know the Son, then they did not know the Father. They did not know God. The God they had come to believe in through their philosophical presuppositions was a different god.

From those heights, Athanasius then plunges down to tell the story of the Word in his creation. The Word, he says, was often known by the saints of the Old Testament as the Lord's Angel (here he refers to passages such as Gen. 48:15–16; 32:24–30) 'because it is He alone who reveals the Father'.[26] However, something quite different happened when the Word took flesh, and Athanasius is emphatic that we should not think 'that, as in former times the Word was used to come into each of the Saints, so now He sojourned in a man'.[27] Far from merely sojourning in a body, the Word assumed the flesh entirely in order to 'make it Word'. And then (at last!) Athanasius explains that he does this by the Spirit: 'we, apart from the Spirit, are strange and distant from God, and by the participation of the Spirit we are knit into the Godhead'.[28]

---

25. *Against the Arians* 3.6.
26. Ibid. 3.13.
27. Ibid. 3.30.
28. Ibid. 3.24.

Discourse 4

The fourth discourse is actually a different work, grafted on to the first three as an appendix. Nevertheless, it is well worth looking at for how Athanasius now turns his guns from Arianism to modalism, that belief that the Father, Son and Spirit are but mere, interchangeable modes or masks worn by the one God.

How should the modalists be answered? Athanasius does, of course, wheel out a number of Old and New Testament texts to show the Son's real and distinct being, but his main answer is initially cryptic. The modalists, he says, 'must be confuted from the notion of a Son, and the Arians from that of a Father'![29] We have seen how the Arian problem was that, by denying the Son, they denied the Father; now Athanasius inverts the argument for the modalists, saying that their problem is that they do not even acknowledge the existence of a real Son beside the Father. And that, he says, is actually worse than what the Arians did:

> those who say that the Son is only a name, and that the Son of God, that is, the Word of the Father, is unessential and non-subsistent, pretend to be angry with those who say, 'Once He was not.' This is ridiculous also; for they who give Him no being at all are angry with those who at least grant Him to be in time.[30]

Also, he maintains, by murdering the Son, modalism murders belief in a real and good creation, for if the Word simply goes out from God as a mode of his being to bring creation into existence, what will happen when the Word returns to God (in the ascension and final handover of the kingdom to the Father)? It is the Word who sustains creation; but if the Word returns into God and ceases to have any existence of its own, creation will cease to exist. It would be as if creation were a momentary expansion within God, soon to be swallowed back up into nothing.

---

29. Ibid. 4.4.
30. Ibid. 4.8.

Life of Antony

At the same time as he wrote *Against the Arians* while in desert exile among the monks, Athanasius wrote his biography of their renowned leader, the then recently deceased hermit Antony. The work turned out to be enormously popular and influential, playing a key role in the conversion of Augustine and in spreading the monastic ideal.

It is the story of a young Egyptian who hears and applies literally Jesus' words to the rich young man 'If you want to be perfect, go, sell your possessions and give to the poor, and you will have treasure in heaven. Then come, follow me' (Matt. 19:21). Yet getting rid of his possessions clearly antagonized the devil, who, concerned by this zeal, appeared to Antony with new levels of temptation. Antony then decided that he needed to get more serious, and so moved out into the desert to live as a hermit under the strictest of ascetic regimes. There he wrestled with demons, prophesied, had visions, performed miracles and acquired such a reputation for holiness that the sick came out to be healed by him and disciples came out to follow him.

The general feel of the work is surprisingly upbeat, with an exhilarating sense of the victory of Christ over evil and the demonic (which are 'like snakes and scorpions to be trodden underfoot by us Christians').[31] It is characteristic Athanasius, who always managed to imbue the darker themes of Christian suffering and self-denial with a golden sense of light and joy. In a letter that announced the Lenten fast to the Christians of Alexandria, for instance, his focus was not on gloomy thoughts of self-denial, but on entering the fast so as to relish Christ as the true feast. For Athanasius, fasting and self-denial were associated with gratitude, with looking away from the sensual pleasures that foster self-love to contemplate God and find joy in him. Even suffering fitted into this for Athanasius, who counselled Christians to embrace sickness and afflictions in hope and as means to dispel lust of self and conform them joyfully into the image of Christ.

For all that, though, it seems that Athanasius did not actually entirely agree with Antony's asceticism (though, because of his

---

31. *Life of Antony* 24.

ATHANASIUS 79

profound respect for Antony, he never even comes close to censoring him). Antony's self-denial was always in danger of veering into anti-materialism, something that Athanasius, with his strong doctrine of creation, could never countenance. In a letter to another monk, he warned that it is the devil who suggests 'under the show of purity' that such bodily things as sexuality are inherently evil. Quite the opposite, said Athanasius: 'All things made by God are beautiful and pure, for the Word of God has made nothing useless or impure.'[32]

Going on with Athanasius

Athanasius has a blunt, simple style of writing; however, he can run off on tangents that are quite off-putting for those trying to get to know him for the first time. For that reason, newcomers should probably skip *Against the Heathen*, which is more difficult, and dive straight into *On the Incarnation*, which SVS provides in an easy translation alongside C. S. Lewis's excellent introduction. For those wanting to go a bit deeper, *Against the Arians* should definitely be the next port of call, and can be found online (at <http://www.ccel.org>) or in the *Nicene and Post-Nicene Fathers* (2nd series, vol. 4).

Thomas Weinandy's *Athanasius: A Theological Introduction* (Aldershot: Ashgate, 2007) is probably the best overall introduction, and has the advantage of being up to date with important changes in scholarly opinion. The now classic introduction to the intricacies of the Arian debate is R. P. C. Hanson's *The Search for the Christian Doctrine of God: The Arian Controversy 318–381* (Edinburgh: T. & T. Clark, 1988). Its scholarship is a little dated and it is quite opinionated, yet it remains the standard.

---

32. Letter 48, *To Amun.*

Athanasius timeline

251?	Antony born
256?	Arius born
296–8	Athanasius born in Alexandria, Egypt
303–5	Emperor Diocletian's 'Great Persecution' of Christianity
311	Renewed persecution in Egypt
312	Conversion of the emperor Constantine to Christianity
318	Arius begins to teach that there was a time when the Son was not
325	Council of Nicea
328	Athanasius appointed bishop of Alexandria
335–7	Athanasius' first exile; writes *Against the Heathen* and *On the Incarnation*?
336	Arius dies
339–46	Athanasius' second exile
354	Augustine born
356?	Antony dies
356–62	Athanasius' third exile; writes *Against the Arians*, letters to Serapion and *Life of Antony*
362	Council of Alexandria
362–4	Athanasius' fourth exile
365–6	Athanasius' fifth exile
373	Athanasius dies

4. LOVING WISDOM
Augustine

The fourth century AD was a tumultuous turning point in history. When it began, the Roman Empire was pagan, and Christians were a persecuted minority. When it ended, Christianity was officially accepted, and pagan sacrifices had been made illegal. It was a century that saw the power of the Roman Empire crumble to such an extent that the next would witness the repeated sackings of once-mighty Rome and the complete collapse of the western half of the empire.

As significant as all this, perhaps, was the birth of Aurelius Augustinus in AD 354. Born of a pagan father, Patricius, and a Christian mother, Monica, he was a true child of his times. His life and writings were inseparable from the events around him. Like Rome, he converted from paganism to Christianity. He soon became a bishop, and thus an official of the empire. And his end, like Rome's, came as the barbarian hordes surrounded the city in which he lay dying.

For almost all his life he lived in a provincial backwater of the empire in North Africa. The city of which he was bishop, Hippo Regius (a seaport on what is now the Algerian coast), was otherwise obscure. Yet, in spite of this, Augustine remains perhaps the most influential Christian thinker outside the Bible. His impact on the West, at least, can scarcely be exaggerated. The Reformation in the sixteenth century, for instance, was in many ways a debate within Augustine's head. Both Rome and the Reformers argued that they were the true heirs of Augustine, and both cited him extensively to prove it. Both Luther and Erasmus were once Augustinian monks. And his influence extends well beyond theology, to psychology and philosophy, to shape the very way in which we in the West tend to think of ourselves. Augustine is deep in our blood; and with many of the ideas that he faced still operating today, it seems that he will continue to be of vital importance.

Unsurprisingly, a mind as titanic as Augustine's was extremely prolific. He produced more than two hundred books and treatises on theological, philosophical and pastoral issues, as well as many hundreds of letters and sermons. Yet the combination of over-whelming profundity and so much material (as well as his cultural distance from us) makes Augustine too daunting a prospect for most readers. This need not be. His style is easy and readable, his thought well expressed. All that is needed as a springboard to engagement with him is a rough sketch of the context and contours of his thought.

The place to start is undoubtedly Augustine's *Confessions*, in which the man himself describes his own early life and his early theological and spiritual journey. That introduces Augustine the man and so many of the key points of his thought. With them in place we can complete the picture by working (in rough chrono-logical order) through the major issues he faced in the second half of his life, after having completed the *Confessions*.

Confessions

Augustine wrote his *Confessions* halfway through his life, as a book about his youth. It is not quite an autobiography, however, at least not in the modern sense. For one thing, there is nothing self-congratulatory about it. And, unlike autobiographies, it is written as a prayer. That (coupled with the title) reveals what kind of book it is. It is a confession to God, both of his own sin, and of God's grace to him. It is his testimony. The unusual feature of this testimony, however, is that after nine 'books' or chapters dealing with his life up until just after his conversion, Augustine then finishes the work with four 'books' on memory, time, biblical interpretation and an exegesis of Genesis 1. No wonder the ending so often leaves readers feeling rather thrown! But how these last four 'books' relate to the first nine is vital to understanding Augustine's purpose.

Book 1

Augustine opens the *Confessions* with a paragraph that really encapsulates the whole work:

> Great are you, O Lord, and greatly to be praised; great is your power, and of your wisdom there is no end. Man, being a part of your creation, longs to praise you. He carries his mortality with him, the sign of his sin, the proof that you thwart the proud. Yet man, as part of your creation, still longs to praise you. You arouse us to delight in praising you, for you have made us for yourself, and our hearts are restless until they find rest in you.[1]

Thus Augustine introduces his central theme, which is to be his and all humanity's journey towards rest in God. It is a deeply Christian paragraph (alluding to Pss 145:3; 147:5; 1 Pet. 5:5; Rom. 10:14), but it is also strongly Neoplatonic. The Neoplatonist tradition (which we will examine below) placed a premium on the notion of the soul's movement towards such rest, and was filled with works written as prayers to God. And having noticed the presence of both traditions here, we have noticed something vital about the mature Augustine who wrote the *Confessions*, whose mind was precisely such a mixture of Christian and Neoplatonic thought.

---

1. *Confessions* 1.1.1. Quotations from the *Confessions* are my translation, although no translation seems able to capture the excitement and vivacity of Augustine's Latin.

Augustine then begins his story with a reflection on his infancy. It is not that he can actually remember it, but he writes of it so that he can start things by proving the sinful guilt of even newborn babies from their radical selfishness. In fact, his description of his entire childhood, of how he would lie, hate, cheat and steal, serves not only as a confession of his own wickedness and self-obsession, but as a refutation of the concept of childhood innocence.

Guilty and sinful he might have been; nevertheless, Augustine believed that even at this early stage his journey towards God was beginning. As a child he loved classical Latin literature. In fact, in many ways his life as described in the *Confessions* is a story of encounters with books. His favourite as a child was Virgil's *Aeneid*, the story of the Trojan hero Aeneas' wanderings after the fall of Troy, and of how he came to Carthage before going on to found what would become Rome. It becomes the model for Augustine's own life, the *Confessions* being his own spiritual version of the *Aeneid* as he describes his own spiritual wanderings, which would also take him from Carthage to Rome.

Book 2

Augustine then pursues the theme of his sinful youth, describing in a highly resonant, compelling and convicting way what it is like to sin. The major event of the book is a minor incident from when he was sixteen, but he uses it as both an example and an opportunity to examine the nature of sin. Along with some friends he stole some pears from a neighbour's tree. It may have been a petty crime, but he later felt it displayed his real self. Here he was, another Adam, stealing forbidden fruit. And why did he do it? It was not that he actually wanted the pears themselves (he cannot remember if he even ate any of them); he simply enjoyed doing something illicit. As he sees it, it perfectly illustrates the human condition: sin uses the law as an opportunity for displaying its natural desire to rebel against the Lord (Rom. 7:7–11). The irony he notices is that, while at the time he thought he was making himself divinely free and happy in putting himself above the law, the reality was that he was doing it only to fit in with and follow his friends, and that it did not, after all, bring happiness.

Book 3
In order to continue his education, he then moved, like Aeneas, to
Carthage (now Tunis). And, like Aeneas, he found love there. For
Aeneas it had been a woman, Queen Dido. Not for Augustine:
during his studies he read the *Hortensius*, by the great Roman orator
and philosopher Cicero, and was greatly attracted by his noble style
of communication. The *Hortensius* is an exhortation to philosophy
(literally, the 'love of wisdom') in which Cicero encourages the
reader to find eternal wisdom. The book turned Augustine into a
philosopher, one who loved wisdom (a love that was truly heartfelt for Augustine, meaning that philosophy, for him, could never
be a purely cerebral affair). And so, writing the *Confessions* many
years later, looking back as a Christian who believed that Christ
is Wisdom (1 Cor. 1:24), he felt that, though he had not known
it at the time, at that moment he had begun his search for Christ.
Therefore he writes of Cicero's *Hortensius*, 'This book changed my
affections, and turned my prayers to you, O Lord.'[2]

Because of his mother's Christianity he began to look for the
wisdom he sought in the Bible. Yet, next to Cicero's rhetorical
panache, the poor Latin translation he used seemed woefully
clunky, and its content (especially the story of Adam and Eve)
just struck him as naive. He had major questions to ask, especially
concerning the nature and body of God and the origin of evil
(questions that would remain key for him throughout his life), but
at that time Christianity did not appear to have any satisfactory
answers.

Instead, he turned to the sinister and feared sect of the
Manichees, who had a more obvious answer to the problem of
evil. The Manichees were followers of the third-century Persian
prophet Mani, a man who believed himself to be the Paraclete
promised by Jesus in John 14 – 16. They saw themselves as basically Christian, though they were strict dualists, holding the body
to be evil and the soul good. As a result, they could not accept
the Creator as being the true and good God, for he had brought
all that was bad (matter) into existence. This meant rejecting the

2. Ibid. 3.4.7.

Old Testament and large parts of the New. Furthermore, they could not believe that Jesus was truly human, or that he had been truly crucified, for it would be impossible to nail a spirit to wood. Instead, they viewed the cross as a symbol for the poor plight of all humanity. Their answer to Augustine's problem of evil, however, was attractively simple: evil exists because matter exists. It was almost as attractive as the fact that, according to their teaching, his soul could remain untarnished by the physical relationship he soon began with a concubine.

Book 4
Augustine's latest ideas were soon put to the test with the death of a dear Manichaean friend. This friend had fallen ill and, while unconscious, had been baptized by some rather sneaky Christians (such things were known to happen in North Africa in those days). When he recovered consciousness, Augustine teased him about this baptism, assuming his friend would find it amusing. Instead, he found that his friend had genuinely been converted, and so, instead of laughing along with Augustine, sternly rebuked him. Soon after, the friend died, leaving Augustine shocked and grieving. Yet when he reflected on his grief, Augustine saw that it stemmed from his error of treating the friendship as if it had been an immortal one, of trying to satisfy himself with his friend instead of with God.

Book 5
Shaken, the bright young Augustine soon began to ask questions that the local Manichees were unable to answer. When this happened, they invariably seemed to advise him to speak to a revered Manichee leader called Faustus, when he next came to town. Yet when Faustus finally arrived and Augustine set about questioning him, Augustine found Faustus was equally unable to provide him with satisfactory answers. With disillusionment in Manichaeism setting in, Augustine moved to Rome in the hope of finding more educated people to question (as well as better students to enhance his career of teaching rhetoric). For the same reasons he then moved on quickly from Rome to Milan, which had become the real seat of the Roman Empire in the west.

In Italy he began to engage with minds of a different calibre to those he had known in provincial North Africa. This led him to a much more sophisticated philosophy than Manichaeism: Neoplatonism. In the third century AD the philosopher Plotinus had offered the Roman world an interpretation of Plato that was picked up by Plotinus' disciple Porphyry as a weapon with which to defend paganism against the rising force of Christianity. (Today the movement is called 'Neoplatonism', though they saw themselves simply as Platonists.) In stark contrast to Manichaean dualism, Neoplatonism was monist. It taught that there is a hierarchy of being, at the top of which is a divine triad: the One, Mind and Soul. These are the most real beings, the most non-bodily and the most good. From them emanates all being. Evil is what lies at the other end of the spectrum. It is, as it were, where light, goodness and being run out, leaving dark, evil nothingness. Evil, in Neoplatonic thought, is a lack of being and goodness.

Despite its pagan and even anti-Christian pedigree, many Christians in the fourth century began to be attracted to this philosophical movement, in that it spoke intelligently of a reality 'not of this world'. One such Christian was Ambrose, the eminent bishop of Milan.

Book 6

As a teacher of rhetoric, Augustine first went to hear Ambrose preach because of the bishop's outstanding reputation as an orator. Soon, however, it was the content and not just the presentation of Ambrose's message that began to impress Augustine. In particular, Ambrose taught that many biblical stories, especially those from the Old Testament, were to be taken symbolically and not literally. With this he was able to give them a sophisticated application that appealed to Augustine. From then on, Augustine was to have a fondness for allegorical readings of literature, a tendency that clearly affects how he means the *Confessions* to be read (for instance, wanting his young act of theft from the pear tree to be interpreted as symbolic of the fall).

Being infinitely more refined than the Christians of North Africa, Ambrose soon began to give Christianity a new appeal in Augustine's eyes. In large part, no doubt, Ambrose was able to make Christianity credible to Augustine because of his own affinity with the Neoplatonism that had begun to fascinate Augustine. He presented a Christianity that looked easily compatible with Plotinus' philosophy.

Book 7

In this intriguing central book of the *Confessions*, Augustine becomes certain of the intellectual superiority of Christianity. What is strange is that he is convinced of it by reading Neoplatonist philosophy. He believed that Neoplatonism had understood all the essential elements of Christianity, with the exception of the incarnation and atonement. It was because of those doctrines that Christianity was the superior philosophy. Thus, just as he believed Cicero had first pointed him towards God, so here he argues that the Neoplatonists taught him about the Word of God.

All this is important for understanding Augustine's theological method, for of course the Neoplatonists had come to their philosophy by reason, not revelation. It also exposes some of the biases and gaps in his theology. Soon after the events of Book 7 he wrote his *Soliloquies*, in which he stated that all he wanted to know was nothing more than 'God and the soul'.[3] Yet what of Christ, of his incarnation and crucifixion? What of the very world? Augustine needed to (and would) become more explicitly Christian in his interests. Yet Neoplatonism would never cease to exercise a strong grip on his mind. His last recorded words were a quotation from Plotinus.[4]

Book 8

In this book Augustine recounts the climax of his long mental, spiritual and moral journey from Cicero to Mani to Plotinus, and finally to Christ. What he makes clear at the beginning of this book is the moral dimension. Through it all he had battled with an addiction to sex that had led to two mistresses and a child. 'Lord

---

3. *Soliloquies* 1.7.

4. 'He is no great man who thinks it a great thing that sticks and stones should fall, and that men, who must die, should die' (cited in P. Brown, *Augustine of Hippo* [London: Faber & Faber, 1967], pp. 425–426).

give me continence, but not yet' was his famous prayer.[5] He real-
ized that he could not even want what he wanted, so enslaved was
he to his passions.

Then he describes the moment of his conversion in the garden of
his house in Milan. As he had earlier displayed his rebellion against
God under a pear tree in a garden, so now he describes his reconciliation to God under a fig tree in a garden. Walking in the garden
(hear the symbolism), crying at his captivity to sin, he heard a voice
repeating the words *Tolle lege* (Take and read). Understanding this to
be a divine command to read the Scriptures, he picked up his copy
of Paul's letters and read the first passage his eye fell on: 'not in
orgies and drunkenness, not in sexual immorality and debauchery,
not in dissension and jealousy. Rather, clothe yourselves with the
Lord Jesus Christ, and do not think about how to gratify the desires
of the sinful nature.'[6] At this, he says, all the darkness of doubt left
him, and his heart was changed towards God.

Book 9
Augustine is then baptized along with a close friend and his own
son. Soon afterwards, however, his mother (who had followed him
to Italy), his son and two close friends all die. This causes him to
write in some detail about Monica, who had been such a dominat-
ing figure in his life. As well as having been a formidable and rather
clingy mother, she had been a staunch Christian who had rejoiced
at the events she had so long prayed for: the conversion and
baptism of her son. Yet here Augustine reveals the surprising fact
that Monica had for years been something of an alcoholic, before
finally managing to deal with her addiction by total abstention.
This enables him to examine addiction to habits.

It may also shed light on a common accusation thrown at
Augustine, that he is 'anti-sex'. It is true that he is generally
unhelpfully negative regarding sex, seeing it as the conduit for
original sin. Yet to a great extent Augustine was reacting to his
own addiction to sex in the same way as Monica had reacted to her

5. *Confessions* 8.7.17.
6. Rom. 13:13–14.

wine habit – with total abstinence. Moreover, for a fourth-century Christian his views were actually quite moderate. It is his prominence more than his stance that has made him appear to be the main perpetrator of all prudery in the West.

Book 10

The narrative section of the work over, Augustine proceeds to describe himself in the present. Up to this point his focus has been on his own life, written as a small mirror image of the story of creation as it is brought back to God from its fallenness. In the last four books he broadens his vision more explicitly to speak of the bigger picture his life had reflected.

He begins with a discussion of human identity as understood through the concept of *memory* (an appropriate starting point, given how much he has recalled in the first nine books). He sees memory as the very root of the self's identity – how it stays itself from moment to moment. The other key elements of the inner self he believed to be the *intellect* and the *will*. He therefore argued that each human mind is composed of an internal triad analogous to the Trinity (he compares memory to God the Father; intellect [logic] to the Son [the Logos]; and will to the Spirit).

At around the same time as writing the *Confessions*, Augustine began composing his seminal work *On the Trinity*. In that work he also illustrated his understanding of the Trinity by comparing the Father, Son and Spirit to (among other things) the different aspects of an individual human mind.

Book 11

From memory Augustine progresses quite naturally to the question of *time* (analysed through an exegesis of Gen. 1 that will occupy the remainder of the work). He acknowledges that time is an especially profound mystery: 'What, then, is time? If no one ask of me, I know; if I wish to explain to him who asks, I know not.'[7] Yet he is impatient with the joke answer to the question 'what was God doing before creation?' ('Preparing hell for those who pry into

---

7. *Confessions* 11.14.17.

such mysteries'). He wanted to take the question seriously. Instead, his answer is that, since time is a part of creation, there was no time 'before' creation. There was no 'before' creation at all. Thus he argued for a model essentially identical to Plato's sharp distinction between time and a timeless eternity. This was clearly appealing for an audience influenced by Neoplatonism; how well it fits with the biblical model is a question that still divides theologians.

Book 12

Having narrated a story of encounters with books (Virgil's *Aeneid*, Cicero's *Hortensius*, the books of the Platonists and finally the Bible), Augustine now begins to work more systematically through Genesis 1. Here he presents the Bible as the book of books, the true classic that stands above all the revered works of Homer and Virgil, the sum and true presentation of wisdom. In one sense Book 12 is Augustine's guide to biblical interpretation (in a word, to 'allegorize'). In another sense it is a refutation of both Platonism and Manichaeism. Against all forms of Platonism, the Bible shows creation being produced by God out of nothing (rather than out of some pre-existing material); against Manichaeism, creation speaks against dualism and all hatred of the physical.

This is probably the point at which to mention Augustine's mature understanding of evil, which so brilliantly denies Manichaean dualism. Augustine asserted that evil cannot be a thing, for every thing has been created by God, and God's creation is good. Instead, evil is a lack of being, like a hole in something, spoiling it, but not having any independent, substantial existence.

Book 13

Augustine ends his *Confessions* by interpreting Genesis 1 as an allegory of the church (e.g. the creation of the firmament on day two he reads as an allegory of Scripture being placed over the church).[8] This leads him through the creation week to finish the

---

8. This particular allegory is a good example of how variegated even single
   lines of Augustine's thought can be: the theological conclusion sounds
   categorically Protestant; the exegesis that gets him there is absolutely not.

Confessions where he had started it: with the theme of rest. His heart had found rest in God, and now he looks forward to the promised rest of the eternal Sabbath.

Life and theology after the *Confessions*

Two years after his conversion Augustine went back to Africa. Returning as an exceptionally able convert from Manichaeism, Augustine was welcomed as an essential asset in the North African church's fight against the sect. As such he was soon forcibly ordained as a presbyter in Hippo (like stealth baptisms, a practice not uncommon in the region at the time). His dreams of a life of philosophical contemplation were shattered. Instead, his new role compelled him to do theology in the service of the church.

Since his conversion he had lived a monastic life, which, until his ordination, had meant ivory-towered isolation. He would remain for the rest of his life in a monastery, living out an austere monastic rule. From that time on, however, the monastery was to serve as a seminary for Africa. Especially after Augustine was consecrated Bishop of Hippo, four years later, he succeeded in importing a constellation of highly talented young men who were then planted as bishops across the province.

Against the Donatists

The church in Hippo faced not only the Manichees, but also the Donatist sect. In fact, the Donatists outnumbered the Catholics in Hippo ('Catholic' at this point simply meant 'ortho-dox', the opposite, not of Protestantism, but heresy). Donatism owed its existence to events of nearly a century before. Prior to Constantine's conversion to Christianity, the emperor Diocletian had instigated a particularly thorough programme for the per-secution of Christianity from 303 to 305. Bishops were asked to hand over copies of the Bible to be burnt, and some complied. And so the troubles began. Some Christians believed that such treachery meant that the guilty bishops were no longer worthy

of being bishops; their authority in the church was voided. As a
result, those they ordained were not truly ordained and those they
baptized were not truly baptized. All their churches were polluted.
In response, 'pure' rival bishops were elected, one of whom, in
Carthage, was called Donatus. The church in Africa had thus been
torn into two halves: the 'ultra-pure' followers of Donatus with
their rival bishops, and the 'corrupted' Catholic rump.

As the ablest theologian in the region, Augustine was saddled
with the task of responding to the claims made by the Donatists.
At one level his reply was deliberately unscholarly. 'His polemic
against the Donatists betrays un unsuspected flair for journalism
. . . He sensed the popular tone of the controversy, and exploited
it with gusto. He will begin his campaign by writing a popular
song.'[9] At another level his response to the 'pure ecclesiology' of
the Donatists was a theology of the church and sacraments that is
still determinative today.

Augustine argued that the church is not a pure society, but must
consist of both wheat and tares until Christ himself separates them
at the end of the age. There is no salvation outside the church, but
the unsaved can also be found inside the church. He agreed that
the true church and the outward church can be distinguished, but
maintained that the two cannot be separated by crude human division, as the Donatists thought, but only by God in final judgment.
In this way he denied the possibility of a perfect denomination or
church.

As for the sacraments, he argued that a sacrament's validity
does not depend on the holiness of the one who administers it.
That misunderstands the nature of a sacrament. Sacraments, he
suggested, are 'visible words'.[10] Words are a type of sign, pointing
us to a reality. Scripture itself, as the word of God, is a sign, pointing us to God. Sacraments are signs of the gift of grace. When we
follow the sign by believing it, we receive the reality of the grace
it points to. The Donatist's mistake, Augustine argued, was to
confuse the sign with the reality.

---

9. Brown, *Augustine of Hippo*, p. 228.
10. *On Christian Doctrine* 2.3.

Within a few years Donatism was officially anathematized, and began to be suppressed. Initially, Augustine was opposed to all compulsion in matters of faith. But when he saw how Donatists crumbled under coercion and rejoined the Catholic church, he revised his position and began writing in defence of the use of force in the subdual of heresy. It was certainly ironic that 'the only Father of the Church to write at length on persecution had himself been a member of a persecuted sect',[11] but then himself began to see force as an instance of much-needed discipline, for 'the LORD disciplines those he loves' (Prov. 3:12).

Augustine's reputation has been severely damaged by the use of his arguments in subsequent church history to sanction all manner of violence against those deemed heretical. However, when, for example, those defending the persecution of the Huguenots in seventeenth-century France appealed to Augustine, they were highly selective in their reading. Augustine's principle commended the loving discipline of a father, and that implied restraint as much as coercion. Torture and capital punishment never applied in his vision.

The City of God

On 24 August 410 Alaric's Visigoths sacked the city of Rome, the symbolic heart of the empire. Culturally, it was a shattering event that left the Romans in a deep state of shock. 'If Rome be lost, where shall we look for help?' wrote Jerome.[12] Suddenly, the province of North Africa was flooded with refugees from Rome, and the people of Hippo were treated to the sight of rich and famous pagan aristocrats walking their streets. Those pagans were vocal in announcing the fact that Rome, which had stood unbreached for 800 years, had fallen swiftly after the official adoption of Christianity. The protection of the old gods had been cast aside, and this, they suggested, was the result. It was a powerful apologetic for a return to classical paganism.

---

11. Brown, *Augustine of Hippo*, p. 242.
12. Letter 123.

In this context Augustine set out his massive counter-apologetic, *The City of God*. The work, however, was far more than a mere reaction or tract for the times. Rather, Augustine used the events of 410 as a platform for a definitive theology of history and politics. His essential point is that the refugees from Rome, living in Africa but hankering to return to the great city, had the right idea. Their mistake was to long for the wrong city: instead, they should long for the heavenly Jerusalem, the City of God. The Christians, he explains, are the ones who understand this, as, like refugees in this world, they ever long for their true heavenly home. It is that heavenly vision that can put the fate of earthly empires like Rome into the correct perspective.

He begins the argument by mercilessly demolishing the theory that the pagan gods had ever offered Rome or their worshippers any protection ('Books' 1–7). He then proceeds to a much more sympathetic discussion of the merits and demerits of Platonism ('Books' 8–10). Then, demolition done, the second half of the work ('Books' 11–22) presents his positive argument for the truth of Christianity. This is done through a chronological overview of all history as described in the Bible, from creation to heaven and hell. Human history, he demonstrates, has from the beginning been a conflict between the City of Man, which is built on love of self, and the City of God, which is built on love of God. This account of the human story was a vital part of the apologetic for Augustine. Roman society had a tendency to venerate antiquity and to be suspicious of novelty, making Christianity unattractive for having appeared so late on the scene. Augustine argued that this was simply not the case: ever since the time of Adam, the City of God had been populated by those who loved God and were saved by the grace of Christ.

The City of God was much more than an apologetic, though. Augustine also wrote it in order to challenge the increasing nominalism of the day. The Christianity he articulated was about political allegiance to the City of God, not political allegiance to the new Christian status quo. And, as relevant today as ever, he wrote to prevent what he called the 'insanity' of confusing any earthly institution with the City of God.

Against the Pelagians

Among the tide of refugees from Rome swept up on the North African coast at Hippo was an austere but brilliant British monk called Pelagius. For a number of years he had taught in Rome, moving in the most exalted circles (circles that included the pope himself), and leading a protest against the rise of nominal Christianity and the decline of Christian morality. He did not remain long in Hippo, but Augustine's ongoing dispute with him and his followers would be the one for which the bishop of Hippo would justly be best known. In Pelagius, Augustine found that he was no longer dealing with the second-rate minds of local sectarians: here was a theological opponent of an entirely different calibre.

Pelagius' beliefs were essentially simple. He believed that each person has the responsibility and the potential to be morally perfect. Such is God's command, and God would not command the impossible. Any suggestion that we are in fact incapable of such perfection he believed would amount to a gross toleration of sin.

From this basic position sprang a small catalogue of ideas. First, he argued that death is a simple biological necessity, not a punishment for sin (for all die, even though some, he believed, had managed to live without sin). Secondly, he maintained that there is no such thing as inherited guilt. When Adam sinned, he alone was punished for his sin. In his commentary on Romans 5, Pelagius took Paul to mean that it is those who copy Adam in his sin who are punished as he was, not that all Adam's posterity are cursed and found guilty through being in Adam. For Pelagius believed we are born innocent, in the same state as Adam before the Fall. If, then, damnation comes through copying Adam, and not by inheriting it from him at birth, salvation likewise comes through copying Christ, and not by receiving it freely from him in a new birth. That is why God gave the Law, so that through obeying it we can achieve the perfection God demands and bring back paradise on earth.

When the theologies of Pelagius and Augustine are compared, Pelagius is popularly touted as the more appealing of the two because of his optimism in humanity and his defence of individual human freedom. Promoting a self-help save-the-planet theology, it is no wonder Pelagius receives the better press. Yet in fact it was Pelagius' theology that was the stern and chilling one. He placed a crushing weight of responsibility on the individual: we each must ensure our own, personal perfection.

Ironically, it was an early work by Augustine, *On the Freedom of the Will*, written against Manichaean determinism, that Pelagius frequently turned to for support. However, by the time Pelagius arrived in Hippo, Augustine was settled in his opposition to Pelagius' theology. Perhaps his experience with Donatism had helped, for Augustine detected a similarity between the two heresies: both believed they could manufacture a perfect church. However Augustine did not believe the two to be equal threats: Pelagianism, by replacing God's grace with human effort, effectively preached a message more pagan/Stoic than Christian.

Strangely, Augustine's anti-Pelagian writings are neglected gems. Because of its recurrent importance in church history, the Augustine–Pelagius debate is normally read rather abstractly and timelessly, or with the sixteenth-century Reformers speaking in Augustine's place. The sad result is that the subtlety of the debate and the beauty of Augustine's response is often missed, leaving it all looking rather sterile and formulaic. Yet Augustine's arguments are quite brilliant, and just as much as the question of truth, it is Augustine's grasp of the warmth and attraction of the gospel as against the cold severity of Pelagius' theology that strikes the reader of the anti-Pelagian writings.

Augustine's first main objection to Pelagius was that he was impossibly individualistic. For Pelagius, each person is essentially an island, a self-defining individual whose own efforts determine his or her own destiny. Augustine clearly saw the injustice and cruelty of this, particularly for the handicapped: if defects are not the result of Adam's sin, but sin is interpreted wholly individually, are the handicapped to be blamed for their own disabilities?

His response was that humankind is not a vast throng of separate individuals, but is instead made up of just two persons: *Adam* and *Christ*. Each of us is merely a member of one of their bodies, dependent for our fate not on ourselves, but on the fate of the head of the body of which we are part. Born from and in Adam, we naturally share both his guilt and nature, irrespective of our own acts: 'we all were in that one man when we all were that one man'.[13] Salvation is to be reborn from and in Christ, to be a part of his Body and so share his righteousness.

Augustine's other main objection was that Pelagius did not understand love as the heart of the gospel. This comes out most clearly in what is probably the most important of the anti-Pelagian writings, *On the Spirit and the Letter*. Pelagius believed that living according to the letter of the Law is all that is required for godliness and salvation. Augustine replied that salvation is given to those who love God, which is not at all the same thing. The letter of the Law cannot stimulate love, and thus it can only deliver damnation (2 Cor. 3:6). Instead of the Law, we need the Spirit to give us the capacity to love.

Augustine defined true love as 'the enjoyment of God for His own sake'.[14] God, he held, is an 'insatiable satisfaction',[15] 'sweeter than all pleasure',[16] and thus we love him, desiring to be rewarded with him, and not something else (he had already demonstrated in the *Confessions* the error of trying to enjoy something in the place of God). Augustine thus saw that Pelagius did not love God at all, but only himself: he was using God in order to escape hell and earn heaven for himself (and 'a man who is afraid of sinning because of Hell-fire, is afraid, not of sinning, but of burning'[17]). It is this that provides the all-pervading winsome tenor of Augustine's theology: that he is a theologian of love. From his student days in Carthage, when he fell in love with the idea of

---

13. *City of God* 13.14.

14. *On Christian Doctrine* 3.10.16. The first book of *On Christian Doctrine* is dedicated to the distinction between 'using' and 'enjoying': we 'use' some things (such as a knife and fork) in order to 'enjoy' other things (the roast beef); enjoyment is delighting in something for its own sake. Ultimately, the only object of true enjoyment is God.

15. Sermon 362.28.

16. *Confessions* 9.1.

17. Letter 145.4.

being in love, through all his addiction to sex, his love of friends and, of course, his love of wisdom, it is love that thrilled his heart and shaped his thinking.[18]

One important caveat regarding Augustine's theology of love: for all its strength as a piece of theology, the exegesis in *On the Spirit and the Letter* is not always accurate. 'Justification' he takes to mean 'being made righteous' – it is the pouring or infusing of the love of God into our hearts (Rom. 5:5); it is not an external declaration of our righteous status, independent of the state of our hearts. For Augustine, to be justified is to be made loving, which happens by faith. By noting this feature at the heart of his anti-Pelagian writings, it can be seen how Augustine sowed the seeds for both the Roman Catholic and Protestant theologies of the sixteenth century.

What, next, of Augustine and Pelagius on human free will? Both believed in free will, though by it each meant a very different thing. Pelagius believed that we are able to choose what or whom to love. In contrast, Augustine believed that our will is governed by what we love. Our freedom is that our wills cannot be forced externally. Thus, without the Spirit, we freely choose to love sin, yet we cannot choose otherwise. It takes the Spirit to work internally in us to give us a new object worthy of love and so free our wills to love God.

Augustine's debate with Pelagianism was to occupy much of the last twenty years of his life, and during this time his own stance changed. When writing *On the Spirit and the Letter* (from 412), he believed, for example, that faith is our work. It is not clearly seen as a gift of God. In the last three years of his life he would retract

---

18. Anders Nygren famously attacked Augustine's theology of love in his
    Agape and Eros (London: SPCK, 1938), arguing that it is more Platonist
    than Christian. Nygren maintained that only the love that gives (*agapē*)
    is truly Christian; the love that desires (*eros*) is actually sinful. John
    Burnaby responded with a magisterial defence of Augustine, arguing that
    Augustine had understood the true nature of Christian love better, that it
    is a desiring love as well as a giving love (*Amor Dei: A Study in the Religion of
    St. Augustine* [London: Hodder & Stoughton, 1938]).

this to argue that our initial faith is indeed a gift.[19] This in turn led him to argue that God must choose to give the gift of faith to some and not others. This final move would be yet another major legacy he would leave to the church in the West, for nobody before him had handled election in the way he had with such unique, intricate articulation.

Finally, and most importantly, Augustine's theology officially triumphed over that of Pelagius (though, of course, Pelagius' ghost has never been completely exorcized from the church). At first Augustine had been seen as an isolated provincial quibbling with a cosmopolitan theologian who commanded widespread support. Yet a year after the bishop's death, in 431, Pelagianism was formally condemned at the Council of Ephesus.

Going on with Augustine

Augustine provides a prime example of what it is like to read a great theologian from the past: both grand and alien, both profoundly right and profoundly wrong (often in the same sentence), he challenges in every way. His great temporal distance from us dares our comfortable and well-worn formulas. Even the mistakes we recognize as characteristic of his age force us to ask what mistakes are characteristic of ours.

Where should the beginner go from here? Undoubtedly to the man himself: the secondary literature on Augustine is bewilderingly immense, and generally the man himself is considerably easier to read than his commentators. The first port of call should definitely be the *Confessions*; after that, *The City of God*, *On Christian Doctrine* and his own small 'systematic theology', the *Enchiridion*, are all near 'musts' for the thinking Christian. *Augustine: Later Works*, Library of Christian Classics (London: SCM, 1955), also contains a collection of highly readable shorter works (*On the Spirit and the Letter*, *On the*

---

19. *On Grace and Free Will* 33.18; *Retractions* 1.23; cf. J. Burnaby, Introduction to *On the Spirit and the Letter*, in *Augustine: Later Works*, Library of Christian Classics [London: SCM, 1955], pp. 189–192.

Trinity and *Homilies on the Epistle of John*), accompanied by excellent explanatory notes. The *Homilies on the Epistle of John* are particularly stirring, bite-sized sermons on his theology of love. After that, the best introduction to Augustine is his definitive biography, which clearly puts his theology in context: Peter Brown's *Augustine of Hippo* (London: Faber & Faber, 1967). A wonderful read.

All in all, Augustine is worth reading, not only because he has been massively influential on subsequent Christian thought, but because he still can be. 'Take and read'!

Augustine timeline

303–5   Emperor Diocletian's 'Great Persecution' of Christianity
312   Conversion of the emperor Constantine to Christianity
354   Born in Thagaste (Souk Ahras in modern Algeria)
371   Studies in Carthage (modern Tunis, Tunisia)
372   Takes a concubine who soon bears him a son, Adeodatus; becomes a Manichee
373   Reads Cicero's exhortation to seek wisdom (*Hortensius*)
376   His unnamed Manichee friend converts to Christianity and dies
383   Moves to teach rhetoric in Rome
384   Moves to Milan, where he meets Bishop Ambrose
386   Converts to Christianity
387   Augustine's Christian mother, Monica, dies
388   Returns to Thagaste to lead a life of philosophical contemplation
391   Forcibly ordained
395   Appointed bishop of Hippo Regius (Annaba in modern Algeria)
397   Starts writing *Confessions*
399   Starts writing *On the Trinity*
410   Alaric's Goths sack Rome
413   Starts writing *City of God*
430   Dies in Hippo

5. FAITH SEEKING UNDERSTANDING
Anselm

When Augustine laying dying in Hippo in 430, Vandal hordes surrounded the city. And for the next few hundred years such Germanic tribes kept Europe so unstable and illiterate that serious theological study was well nigh impossible. Thus no truly great theological mind emerged again until the eleventh century, in Anselm.

Anselm's life

Anselm was born in 1033 in the shadow of the Matterhorn, in the northern Italian town of Aosta. Little is known of his youth, but his mother seems to have been the one who held the home together, for Anselm and his father, Gundulf, cordially disliked each other. When she died, it did not take long for things to fall apart, and, aged twenty-three, Anselm walked out. For three years he wandered Burgundy and France, perhaps looking for a life, perhaps sampling it in ways not possible back at home.

In 1059 he arrived at the Benedictine abbey of Bec in Normandy.

It was not that he was interested in becoming a monk; it was that the monastery had an external school run by Lanfranc, the abbey's prior, and Lanfranc's scholarly reputation was magnetic. However, it did not take long for the appeals of the monastery to take hold, and within a year Anselm entered the abbey as a novice monk.

The all-embracing life of the cloister was perfectly suited to Anselm, who was soon known for his severe personal austerity, seriousness and precision. The lack of food and sleep also induced hallucinatory experiences that were to be part and parcel of his mystical bent. When he had arrived at Bec, Anselm had had minimal education, but his intense intellectual brilliance soon won him a name as an inspirational teacher, as exacting in his thought as he was in his lifestyle.

Anselm was no cold fish, though. Again and again contemporaries spoke of his exuberance in conversation and his winning charm. Yet his personal warmth was more than temperamental: it was an expression of his novel understanding of friendship. In the eleventh century, friendship was viewed in quite business-like terms, as an alliance entered into to achieve some common purpose; Anselm saw friendship as a union of souls, and so a fore-taste of the harmony of heaven.

As such he would write to fellow monks describing the passionate embraces and kisses they had and would share. And he would do so in language so physical it makes for embarrassing reading: 'my arms stretch out to your embraces; my lips long for your kisses'. Unsurprisingly, many have therefore wondered if Anselm was homosexual. That is quite possible, but it does not explain the rationale for the kissing and embracing. Anselm wrote of such things in open letters so that others might learn from the practice, so it is clear that Anselm was not describing forbidden yearnings and acts; moreover, he could write them to people he had never met. It was that he viewed physical embraces as the external signs of the union of souls found in friendship.

The world that Anselm had left outside the monastery was one of feudalism and strict social hierarchy, but the spiritual world he had entered was, if anything, just as tiered. At the top of the chain of being was, of course, God; just below God sat Mary, devotion to whom was gathering strength (something Anselm, who was

prepared to refer to Mary as 'reconciler of the world', was instru-
mental in assisting); below her were the other saints, who were
also used as intermediaries; they, along with the angels, existed
above humans on earth, who existed above animals, plants and,
finally, the inanimate.

It was also a world of deliberate, cultivated introspection as
monks worked to fill themselves with the horror of self and the
knowledge of God. But with no sense of spiritual security underlying the introspection, it was a theological system full of dread. The
sense of sheer terror at the thought of committing any sin can be
seen when, one day, Anselm ate pickled eel before remembering
that eating raw flesh was against the Mosaic Law. Seeing his deep
distress, his friend Eadmer consoled him, saying 'The salt has
removed the rawness of the flesh,' to which Anselm responded,
'You have saved me from being tortured by the memory of sin.'[1]
Almost the only hope of salvation was through the committed
monastic life, and so Anselm wished that everyone would become
a monk or a nun. Few would be saved, and most of those, he was
sure, would be monks or nuns. Even then, the monks and nuns
had to be resolute in their abandonment of the world. As he wrote
to one nun:

> Let all your conversation be in the cloister, not in the world. This world
> is nothing to you, nothing but dung, if you wish to be a nun and spouse
> of God . . . Do not visit your relatives, they do not need your advice, nor
> you theirs. Your way of life is cut off from theirs. Let all your desire be
> for God.[2]

After Anselm had spent just three years in the monastery,
Lanfranc moved on (ultimately to become archbishop of
Canterbury), and, despite Anselm's inexperience, his aptitude for
the life and his intellectual gifts meant he was elected to succeed

1. Eadmer, *The Life of St Anselm: Archbishop of Canterbury*, ed. and tr.
   R. W. Southern (London: T. Nelson & Sons, 1962), vol. 2, p. xiii.
2. R. W. Southern, *Saint Anselm: A Portrait in a Landscape* (Cambridge:
   Cambridge University Press, 1990), p. 165.

Lanfranc as prior. Thus the monastery's reputation grew, with Anselm (in addition to his teaching and official duties) writing such key works as his *Monologion* and *Proslogion*, and taking up his role as counsellor-by-letter to the rulers of Europe. It was not just Anselm's abilities that won him the influence and renown he soon had: during this time, William, Duke of Normandy, invaded England, giving all those in Normandy an influence far beyond what they had previously enjoyed.

His conscientiousness meant that, fifteen years after being appointed prior, when the abbot died, Anselm was elected to succeed him and so be father to the whole monastery. He could hardly have been less pleased: upon his election, he threw himself prostrate on the floor, crying to be freed from the burdens of that office. For, where Lanfranc had been an exceptionally gifted administrator and street-smart political operative, Anselm was an abysmal administrator with no understanding of finance and no political savvy. Not that Anselm himself saw any of that as a deficiency: he did not want to be wise in the ways of the world, for such things were distractions from the monastic life and he genuinely longed to be rid of them. And his fears were confirmed: after his phase of impressive theological productivity as prior, the next fifteen years saw very little theological output as administrative duties used up his time.

Worse was to come as, when visiting England in 1093, King William II, the ruthless and fiery son of the Conqueror, compelled Anselm to succeed his old master, Lanfranc, as archbishop of Canterbury. This would mean even more distractions than dealing with a few monks. Again Anselm was in tears at the prospect, so distraught that he gave himself a nosebleed as he protested to the king his inability. The king tried to force the archbishop's pastoral staff into Anselm's clenched fist, something that required the help of a number of bishops who were with him. Anselm was then lifted up, carried into the church and acclaimed archbishop.

Once again his fears became reality as he found dealing with a foreign country and a high-handed king extremely taxing. He tried to write his next major work, *Cur Deus Homo*, but hardly had any time to do so, making it a project that would drag on for years. What made things especially difficult was the king's insistence on exercising control over the church, meaning that Anselm was unable without the king's permission to reform the church as he wished to.

After a while he decided to seek the advice of the pope in Rome. The king refused to let him go, but eventually Anselm just went, to which the king responded by barring him from re-entry to the country. It was with a glimmer of hope, then, that Anselm arrived in Rome in 1098 and asked the pope to release him from the burden of his office. The pope flatly refused, instead ordering him to go to the Council of Bari in southern Italy where representatives of the Greek and Latin churches were to meet in an attempt to heal the great schism of East and West that had opened up a few decades earlier. There Anselm was instructed to defend the West's view that the Spirit eternally proceeds from the Son as well as the Father. In preparation, Anselm spent a happy summer in the little hill village of Liberi above Capua, where he also completed *Cur Deus Homo* (and miraculously opened a well for the village). All in all, with time spent in Capua, Bari and Rome, it was a blissful exile from the stresses and duties of Canterbury.

Then, in 1100, King William was shot while hunting and his younger brother, now Henry I, invited Anselm to return. With a heavy tread, the archbishop made his way back to a situation that would be every bit as strained as it had been under William II. Soon Anselm was after the pope's advice again (and there was a new pope now, whom Anselm hoped might be more amenable to letting him off the hook), and history repeated itself, with Anselm leaving and King Henry refusing to allow him to return. This time, Anselm tried opening proceedings to get Henry excommunicated, but the pope went over his head to resolve the situation very awkwardly, forcing Anselm to make his way back to Canterbury.

As archbishop, Anselm did manage to write a number of other more minor works as well as *Cur Deus Homo*, though his years were increasingly distracted and troubled. His health declined, forcing him to be carried around in a litter for his last years, and then, on 21 April 1109, he died peacefully at Canterbury, surrounded by his monks.

Anselm's thought

In Anselm's day it had long been traditional for theology to be done meditatively in the monasteries; yet a phenomenon was on the rise: the new secular schools of theology, where theology would be learnt through debate. It was these schools (*schola*) that would host the scholastic style of doing theology (something we will meet properly in the next chapter).

Anselm has sometimes been called the father of scholasticism. Yet Anselm was a monk. And, while later material of his, such as *Cur Deus Homo*, is written in a dialogue form that in some faint ways can resemble scholastic debate, his whole tone and approach to theology is that of the monastery, not the schools. He never sought (as the greatest scholastic theologian, Thomas Aquinas, would) to lay out the whole sweep of his thought; instead, Anselm wrote his theology a piece at a time as monks asked him to respond to their questions. And when he wrote it, it was clearly designed to be read slowly and meditatively. This is something lost in English translations, for the elegance of Anselm's Latin, with its rhymes and rhythms, simply does not translate. But the beauty of Anselm's style was important and deliberate. Anselm believed that only beautiful words are fitting to describe God, whom he saw as Beauty itself, and he wrote his theology as an experimental exercise in the contemplation and enjoyment of that Beauty. It was the monastic style, and Anselm excelled at it.

Anselm also had his own intellectual agendum, a project he called 'faith seeking understanding', which would characterize all his theology. By it he meant that he would use unaided reason to investigate and prove the truths of the Christian faith, and would do this without ever having to fall back on to what the Bible, the church or any Christian theologian had said. God, he held, is Reason itself, and therefore Christian doctrines must be rational; furthermore, God created humans rational, and therefore those doctrines must be explicable and defensible by reason – even reason alone. Anselm thus believed that by pure reason he could prove God's existence, attributes and triune being as well as the fact that God had to send a God-man to die voluntarily in our place so that we might be saved.

Yet how, one might wonder, is this *faith* seeking understanding? By 'faith' Anselm did not mean a basic assent to the truth of Christianity, but an active love for God. It is this love of God that seeks to know God. *That* is faith seeking understanding. Moreover, this love for God is what enables us to reason purely, Anselm maintained, for without love for God we become irrational, foolish and blind.

That said, while Anselm himself found his love of God compelling him to seek a greater knowledge of God, he did not think that 'faith seeking understanding' meant that his theology was only for those who already had faith. It is not as if he saw faith as the universal prerequisite for understanding God (a belief some later scholars have mistakenly credited him with). Rather, he believed that by his reason alone he could persuade unbelievers of the truths of the Trinity, the incarnation and so on.

What exactly 'faith seeking understanding' looked like we can now see as we turn to look at the *Monologion*, the *Proslogion* and, finally, *Cur Deus Homo*.

Monologion

During his time as prior of Bec, some of the monks apparently asked Anselm to write on 'how one ought to meditate on the divine essence'. The result was the *Monologion* (Soliloquy), or, as it was originally titled, 'A Pattern for Meditation on *the Reason* of Faith' (my emphasis). One thing the monks had stipulated for this meditation was that 'absolutely nothing in it would be established by the authority of Scripture'; all would be worked out by reason alone.[3] Thus Anselm opens the *Monologion* with the following:

> If anyone does not know, either because he has not heard or because
> he does not believe, that there is one nature, supreme among all existing
> things, who alone is self-sufficient in his eternal happiness, who through
> his omnipotent goodness grants and brings it about that all other things
> exist or have any sort of well-being, and a great many other things that

---

3. *Monologion*, Prologue. All quotations of Anselm taken from Thomas
   Williams's translation, *Anselm: Basic Writings* (Indianapolis: Hackett, 2007).

we must believe about God or his creation, I think he could at least
convince himself of most of these things by reason alone, if he is even
moderately intelligent.[4]

So his aim is to persuade 'anyone [who] does not know, either
because he has not heard or because he does not believe'. Or, as he
put it later, he was 'adopting the role of someone who, by reasoning silently within himself, investigates things he does not know'.[5]

He starts the investigation by arguing that there must be a
supremely good being, the source of all good. Being supremely
good, this being must be supremely great, and being supremely
great, this being 'must therefore be living, wise, powerful and
all-powerful, true, just, happy, eternal, and whatever similarly it is
absolutely better to be than not to be'.[6]

Having established this, Anselm finds it remarkably easy to go
on to specify what this supremely great being must be like. First,
it is obvious that this being cannot have been brought into being
by any other being, or else that other being would be greater still,
which would contradict the supreme being's supreme being. This
being, then, must exist because of itself, and all other things must
exist because of it. Therefore it must have created all other things
out of nothing.

But as well as never having been brought into existence, this
being cannot cease to exist (for 'he who assuredly is the supreme
good will not perish voluntarily. But if, on the other hand, he is
going to perish unwillingly, then he is not supremely powerful'[7]).
This being must be omnipresent, since nothing can have any
independence from him. He must exist beyond time, for 'he exists
as a whole all at once in all places and times'.[8] Being supreme,
it is impossible that he could ever be acted upon passively;
he must, therefore, be impassible. Also, being perfect, there is

4. *Monologion* 1.
5. *Proslogion*, Prologue.
6. *Monologion* 15.
7. Ibid. 18.
8. Ibid. 21.

nothing greater for the supreme being to become (and he would never become anything less than supreme); therefore he must be immutable.

From this quite standard exploration of the divine attributes or characteristics, Anselm then moves on to an entrancing study of the Trinity as Augustine understood it (the difference being that Anselm is going to prove all by reason). The first move is made off the back of the logical conclusion that the supreme being must be the creator of all things. That is, in order to be the Creator, the supreme being must first consider or say within himself what he is going to create. But this consideration or utterance in the supreme being's mind cannot itself be a creature. It is itself the supreme being. More, since this utterance is itself the supreme being, it cannot consist of many words, for the supreme being must be a 'simple' being. (The 'simplicity' of God is important throughout Anselm's thought. It entails that God does not *have* multiple 'parts' like justice, life, wisdom etc., else he would depend on those things. Rather, he *is* those things. And since he does not have such 'parts' on which he must depend, God is a simple being as opposed to a composite being. In this case this means that God cannot 'have' words; he *is* Word.)

So far, Anselm realizes, what has been said about this utterance or Word of God could make it sound as if the Word exists only as God's preparation for creation. It is how God considers what he going to create, meaning that there would be no Word if creation did not exist. However, Anselm says, God is not ignorant (that would be an imperfection); thus he must know himself; thus he must consider or utter himself in his mind. Thus there must be a Word of God whether or not God decides to create. And because God is simple, it cannot be that God has one Word by which he utters himself, and another Word by which he utters creation. There must be one Word by which he does both.

Next, Anselm argues, because the Word of God cannot be a created being *made* by God, he must be *born* of God: not a creature, but God's own offspring and likeness. If then God has an offspring, which is more fitting: to speak of God as Father or as Mother? Surely, Anselm says, 'since the paternal cause always in some way precedes the maternal', it is more appropriate to speak

of God as Father, for God is the very first, most primary being.[9]
As for the Word as offspring: is it more fitting to speak of the
Word as God's Son or God's Daughter? Since the Word is the
very likeness of the Father, surely the Word should be called the
Son, for no offspring is more like a father than a son, reasons
Anselm.

How else might we speak of the Father and the Son? It is
also reasonable and fitting, Anselm suggests, to call the Father
'memory', for as he knows himself he must remember himself.
But how does he remember himself? By his contemplation of
himself. That is, in his Word who can also then be described as
the Father's 'Wisdom'. Then, out of God's self-understanding and
remembrance must proceed his love for himself. Again, like the
Word, this love cannot be a created thing; it must be the supreme
being itself. But neither can it be construed as another Son, for it
is the mutual love of the Father for the Son, breathed out by both.
And how should we best refer to this love? Being 'breathed out'
(*spiratur*) by both the Father and the Son, he must most fittingly be
called the Spirit (*Spiritus*).

There are many questions one might ask of this whole exercise.
Why, for instance, are God's Word and God's Love personalized
and given such prominence, and not his justice, power, truth or
goodness? Yet perhaps the answer to any such question is rather
obvious: all has been deduced by reason, and the God that reason
has deduced is the God of the Western, Latin church (where the
Spirit proceeds from both the Father and the Son), or more specifically, the God described by Augustine (whose triune being can
be compared to a person's memory, understanding and love). No
surprise there.

Proslogion
Once the *Monologion* was published, Anselm began to have misgiv-
ings about it. It was not that he thought there was anything wrong
with it; it just struck him as unnecessarily complex. It was, as he

9. Ibid. 42.

put it, 'a chaining together of many arguments'; and so he began
to search for

> a single argument that needed nothing but itself alone for proof, that
> would by itself be enough to show that God really exists; that he is the
> supreme good, who depends on nothing else, but on whom all things
> depend for their being and for their well-being; and whatever we believe
> about the divine nature.[10]

It was a tall order. For this single, master argument that Anselm
was after would need to prove not only the existence of God,
but '*whatever* we believe about the divine nature'. Nevertheless,
the search for this super-argument became an obsession with
him. Anselm found himself unable to eat, sleep or concentrate
in chapel. He began to conclude that the whole idea must be a
temptation from the devil. Yet he found he could not let the idea
go. Then, suddenly, during a middle-of-the-night service, it came
to him.

Originally, he wrote the argument down under the title 'Faith
seeking understanding' – it was, after all, the crown of that whole
project of his – but later renamed it the *Proslogion* (Address). Where
the *Monologion* took the form of a soliloquy, the *Proslogion* is an
address to God. Yet the purpose of both is the same. That is, that a
complete doctrine of God 'could be proved by necessary reasons,
independently of the authority of Scripture'.[11] In the *Monologion*
this had been done by adopting the role of an unbeliever working
out the truth by reason. In the *Proslogion* it is done by a believer
proving the irrationality of the fool who says in his heart, 'There
is no God.'

Anselm's argument in the *Proslogion* was built on a formula of
the Roman Stoic philosopher Seneca, who had described God as
being 'that than which nothing greater can be thought'.[12] With this

---

10. *Proslogion*, Prologue.

11. *On the Incarnation of the Word* 6.

12. Immanuel Kant referred to Anselm's argument as the 'ontological
    argument' (without, it seems, ever having read the *Proslogion*), and that is

as his starting point and most basic definition of God, Anselm believed he could convince the atheist fool of his irrationality. The argument goes as follows: the fool who denies God's existence will be able to understand that basic definition of God as 'that than which nothing greater can be thought'. It is a simple concept, that God is a being so great it is simply impossible to think of a greater being. All the atheist need do at this stage is understand that definition of God.

So far, then, 'that than which nothing greater can be thought' can be seen to exist in the understanding of the atheist. However, if 'that than which nothing greater can be thought' existed *only* in his understanding, then it would be quite possible to think of a greater being, that is, a being who existed not only in the understanding but also in reality. But if it is at all possible to think of any greater being, then the atheist cannot have 'that than which nothing greater can be thought' in his understanding. And so, if he does really have 'that than which nothing greater can be thought' in his understanding, then that being must also exist in reality. For it is greater to exist in reality than merely in the understanding.

Furthermore, if we were ever able to think of 'that than which nothing greater can be thought' not existing, then, again, it would be possible to think of a greater being, a being so great that 'it cannot even be thought not to exist'.[13] In other words, 'that than which nothing greater can be thought' must be a being who could not fail to exist. Thus when the fool had said in his heart 'There is no God,' he had imagined a contradiction, that this being that cannot not exist does not exist. Thus he shows that he is stupid and a fool.

It is Anselm's argument for the existence of God (chs. 2–4 of the *Proslogion*) that has received the most attention. However, Anselm's goal in the *Proslogion* had been to prove not only the existence of God, but 'whatever we believe about the divine

---

how it is usually referred to. However, since there are today a number of variations of the ontological argument, I will speak simply of 'Anselm's argument', as his contemporaries did.

13. *Proslogion* 3.

nature'. The rest of the *Proslogion* (chs. 5–26) is therefore dedicated to establishing what we can know about God, given that God is 'that than which nothing greater can be thought'.

Anselm shows that the definition 'that than which nothing greater can be thought' has a remarkable ability to generate descriptions (or prescriptions) of what God must be like. This is for a very simple reason: if God is 'that than which nothing greater can be thought', then God must be 'whatever it is better to be than not to be'.[14] Thus, for example, God must be omnipotent, otherwise we would be able to think of a being that is greater than he. In the same way, God must be just, truthful, happy, impassible, unchanging, non-bodily and so on.

Of course, in order to establish that God is all these things, Anselm has to rely on what he believed were universally self-evident standards of what it is better or greater to be than not to be. And some of those standards seem to have troubling implications: if, for example, it is absolutely better to be non-physical and non-bodily than physical and bodily, why were we created as physical, bodily beings, and why is the Christian hope a bodily one?

The other difficulty with the attributes created by the definition of God as 'that than which nothing greater can be thought' is that they are often apparently self-contradictory. For example, it has been shown that God must be both omnipotent and just. But if God is just, then he cannot be unjust or lie, and that seems to be a limitation on his power. Anselm thus spends the bulk of the rest of the work arguing that such contradictions are not real but only apparent. To the question of whether God's inability to lie or be unjust is a limitation on his power, for example, Anselm poses the counter-question 'Or is the ability to do these things not power but weakness?'[15] Another problem is how God could be both merciful and impassible, 'For if you are impassible, you do not feel compassion.'[16] Anselm's answer is that God does not *feel* merciful even though we do receive mercy from him. And we receive mercy

---

14. Ibid. 5.
15. Ibid. 7.
16. Ibid. 8.

from him because he is just, and his justice requires that he must demonstrate his goodness in sparing some of the wicked (as well as demonstrating his justice by punishing others who are wicked).

Gaunilo's 'Reply on Behalf of the Fool'
Anselm's argument in the *Proslogion* works on most readers like a confusing optical illusion that flicks between two quite different images. The mind cannot decide if Anselm is playing word games or plumbing the depths of profundity. It is a question that keeps theologians and philosophers in work to this day.

One early critic who thought that Anselm was trapped in an unreal web of words was an otherwise unknown monk called Gaunilo, who wrote 'Reply on Behalf of the Fool', arguing that Anselm had proven nothing to the fool. In it Gaunilo satirized Anselm's argument by setting out to prove the existence of an island 'than which no greater can be thought': 'this island', he wrote, 'exists in your understanding, and since it is more excellent to exist not merely in the understanding, but also in reality, this island must also exist in reality'.[17] In other words, it is absurd to think that we can extrapolate from what we imagine in our minds to what exists in reality, for we are perfectly capable of imagining non-existent things in our minds.

Anselm was so unshaken by this answer that he wrote a casual rejoinder to Gaunilo, and stipulated that the exchange be published as an appendix to the *Proslogion*. Clearly, Anselm thought, Gaunilo's reply only showed the resilience of his original argument. It is hard to see quite where Anselm felt Gaunilo had gone wrong, but it seems to be that he thought there was a crucial difference between his being 'than which no greater can be thought' and Gaunilo's island 'than which no greater can be thought'. And that is that where an island by its very nature could fail to exist, 'that than which nothing greater can be thought' cannot not exist, for then we would be able to think of a greater being, and 'that than which nothing greater can be thought' would no longer be 'that than which nothing greater can be thought'.

---

17. Gaunilo's 'Reply on Behalf of the Fool' 6.

Whether or not Anselm was successful in answering Gaunilo, the fact is that, within a century or so, few found his argument to be persuasive any more. Perhaps that is because the whole edifice is built upon a concealed Platonic presupposition, and Plato's time as the most influential philosopher was almost over. The presupposition was that there are degrees of being, and that it is greater to have 'more' being than less. To Anselm that was self-evident, but today most people do not share that presupposition. To us, pigs do not exist 'more' than flying pigs just because flying pigs exist only in our minds. To us, flying pigs simply do not exist. And the argument would be even less compelling in a Buddhist culture where being is something that it is better to have less of.

The presuppositions of anyone using the argument clearly must affect its conclusions. How do we know what it is better or greater to be than not to be? Certainly, Anselm's idea of greatness is not everyone's. For him it was unquestionably greater to be impassible than passible, but few philosophers today would agree. But perhaps it is the very availability of the argument to be used by all that has ensured its enduring appeal. For Anselm's argument can be used alongside almost any presuppositions to prove the existence of any supreme being, whether that be the Christian God, Allah, Brahman or the Great God Om.

Cur Deus Homo

When Anselm became archbishop of Canterbury, there remained one key area of the Christian faith he had not yet 'proved': the incarnation. And the more Anselm's horizons had widened beyond the monastery at Bec, the more he saw the necessity of attending to it. Judaism, with its denial of the incarnation, was perceived to be on the rise. Certainly, there was an increasingly large and vocal Jewish community in England, and its rabbis were putting forward such intelligent arguments against the possibility of an incarnation that Christendom, having undergone centuries of cultural stagnation, felt itself to be on the intellectual back foot. There were a number of conversions to Judaism. Even one well-known bishop converted. And then, in 1095, the pope called for the first crusade. It was a time when Christendom wanted to be confident about what distinguished its faith from Islam and Judaism.

Thus Anselm began work on his apologia for the incarnation, *Cur Deus Homo* (Why God [Became] a Man). Its aim, he said, would be

> to prove by necessary reasons – leaving Christ out of the picture, as
> if nothing concerning him had ever taken place – that it is impossible
> for any human being to be saved apart from Christ . . . and that it was
> necessary that the purpose for which human beings were made should
> in fact be achieved, but only through the agency of a God-man, and
> that it was necessary that everything we believe about Christ should take
> place.[18]

Anselm would rationally defend the incarnation so that, even if we had never heard of Christ or did not believe in him, reason alone would prove that God had to become incarnate and die for us. And not only would he prove its rational necessity; he would display the beauty of God's purpose in the incarnation to answer the charge that the very thought of God becoming incarnate is an insult to the divine dignity.

The work is framed as a dialogue between Anselm and a favourite pupil of his, named Boso. Boso plays the part of a (very gentle) devil's advocate, posing the questions he thinks unbelievers would pose; Anselm answers; then Boso heartily agrees with what Anselm has said before going on to pose the next question.

Book 1
Anselm begins by demonstrating the orderly beauty of God's arrangement:

> For it was fitting that just as death entered the human race through the
> disobedience of a human being, so too life should be restored by the
> obedience of a human being. It was fitting that just as the sin that was
> the cause of our damnation had its origin from a woman, so too the
> author of our justice and salvation should be born of a woman. And it
> was fitting that the devil, who through the tasting of a tree defeated the

---

18. *Cur Deus Homo*, Preface.

human being whom he persuaded, should be defeated by a human being through the suffering on a tree that he inflicted.[19]

Boso's response is that beauty itself is not persuasive to unbelievers, who need to be shown the logical necessity of such an arrangement. This is especially so, he says, since unbelievers (Jews are implied) argue that if God is omnipotent he could simply have willed salvation without having to undergo the indignity of becoming incarnate. If he could not, then surely he is not omnipotent.

Dealing with this demand takes up most of the work, but Anselm feels he can also respond to the underlying assumption that the act of incarnation must be demeaning to God: 'when we say that God was subject to lowliness or weakness, we do not understand this according to the sublimity of his impassible nature but according to the weakness of the human substance he bore'.[20] In other words, and quite simply, God's divinity remains untarnished by Jesus' lowly humanity.

Before going on to look at the logical necessity for the incarnation, Anselm wanted to remove an option that most educated Christians in his day would have used as their answer to why God became man. For centuries the traditional view had been that when Adam and Eve obeyed the devil as he tempted them, they had made themselves (and all humanity in them) his subjects. The devil, from then on, had a just lordship over them, and assumed he had a just lordship over their descendant, Christ. However, Christ never followed the devil and so never was his subject. Thus when the devil tried to exercise lordship over Christ by condemning him to death (as he had a right to do over his own subjects), his overreaching abrogated his right to be lord over humanity at all, and so humanity was freed from the devil's power by the death of Christ. On this view, then, Christ's death was a ransom, paid to the devil to buy off his rights over humanity.

Anselm felt that this approach was entirely wrong-headed. As he saw it, when the devil tempted Adam and Eve, he had simply

---

19. Ibid. 1.3.
20. Ibid. 1.8.

sinned against God, the true Lord over humanity, and an act of sin could never confer rights of any sort. The devil was a mere rebel and thief, with no rights and no lordship over humanity.

Why, then, the incarnation, if not to pay off the devil? Anselm begins by explaining that humanity was created by God to be happy, but that that happiness can be achieved only through humanity's total submission of heart and life to God. Such is God the true Lord's due, and anything less is sin. Sin, then, is essentially the dishonouring of God. Yet this is precisely what humanity is guilty of, and for this reason we have forfeited the happiness for which we were created.

So far the unbeliever (Jew) is clearly expected to agree. But, says Anselm, God could not simply forgive humanity. That would deny his justice, which demands that the outrage of sin be dealt with appropriately. And that is because God's honour should not and cannot be violated. His will (and so honour) is as inescapable as the heavens above, so that if a creature 'flees from God's commanding will, he runs into God's punishing will'.[21]

God, then, cannot just forgive. Something else must happen if humanity is to enjoy the happiness for which we were created. Yet at this point Anselm inserts what to modern readers looks like a bizarre sidetrack, discussing how God created human beings to make up for the number of angels who fell. Weird and irrelevant it may appear to us, but for Anselm it is an important question concerning the reason for which humanity was created. As Anselm sees it, the spaces left in the heavenly city by the fall of the devil and his angels must be made up, and thus God creates humanity and elects a certain number of humans to fill the gaps. In fact, he will elect more humans than there are spaces to fill so that humans can have their own purpose, rather than just being substitute angels. And, Anselm adds, it is important that there be more elect humans than fallen angels, for if there were a mere one-to-one correspondence, each saved human would know that he had replaced a fallen angel, and so would sin by rejoicing over another's downfall.

---

21. Ibid. 1.15.

This rather mechanical view of the purpose and election of humans proves to be highly revealing of Anselm's view of the relationship between God and man. Here, God's plan in creation is to make humans like angels, in being subject only to himself. But that means that God's adoption of us as children, our being treated as anything other than mere servile creatures, and any idea of close fellowship with him is entirely absent from Anselm's thinking. Anselm's usual picture of the relationship between God and man is that of a feudal lord and his serfs.

With that picture in mind, Anselm resumes his main argument: humans owe all to God, but have not given him their due all. As such, they now owe God a recompense. But since we already owe God our all, there is nothing left for us to give God as a recompense. Indeed, our plight is worse even than that. Anselm asks Boso if he would sin to preserve the whole creation. Boso nobly says he would not, which Anselm takes as proof that the cost of sin is worth more than all creation. Thus something more than all creation must be given to God in recompense for sin.

However, the question then arises: If we are so completely unable to pay that recompense, surely God cannot hold us accountable for not paying it? Anselm disagrees, likening us to a servant who throws himself into a deep pit he had been warned to avoid so as to make himself incapable of doing a task his master had commanded. The servant, of course, is incapable of doing the required task, but that does not mean the master will hold him guiltless for his failure; rather, he will punish him doubly, for his failure to do the task, and for his failure to avoid the pit. His inability is his own fault.

Anselm's conclusion to Book 1 is that if Christ did not come to save us, then we would be unable ever to enjoy the happiness for which we were created. Our sin has run us into God's punishing will, and there is nothing we ourselves can do to pay the recompense we must pay to avoid it. Yet it is not as if God would leave us in that state. Some humans must attain happiness, or else God's plan in creating them would be thwarted and God would be shown to have failed, which is impossible. Thus, while God cannot simply forgive us, neither can he fail to show us mercy. The need for Christ is clear.

Boso (unsurprisingly persuaded), then says, 'Now I want you
to lead me further, so that I understand on the basis of rational
necessity that all the things the Catholic faith requires us to believe
about Christ if we want to be saved must be true.'[22]

Book 2
Anselm has established (1) that humankind owes to God a recompense for sin worth more than all creation; (2) that we cannot
pay it; and (3) that God cannot fail to complete what he began in
creating a humanity not made to die but to be happy in enjoying
God. Anselm's conclusion is that there must be 'someone who in
payment for human sin gives God something greater than everything other than God'.[23] But what is greater than everything other
than God? Only God himself. Thus only God can make the recompense. And yet it is man who owes the recompense. Man must
pay it; only God can pay it.

Anselm sees that, by logical deduction, he has proved that a
God-man is necessary for the salvation of humanity that God's
own justice to himself requires. Only one who in his own person
is perfect God and perfect man can fulfil man's obligation to God
and God's obligation to himself.

But Anselm must go further than this if he is to prove 'on the
basis of rational necessity that *all* the things the Catholic faith
requires us to believe about Christ if we want to be saved must
be true'. He starts with the conception and birth of the God-
man. Anselm maintains that the God-man would have to take his
humanity from a virgin, for God would only do what is best and
most fitting for him to do, and to be conceived of a virgin would
be 'purer and more honorable' than to be conceived in the ordin-
ary way:

> There are four ways in which God can make a human being: from a man
> and a woman, as everyday experience shows; or from neither a man nor
> a woman, as he created Adam; or from a man without a woman, as he
> made Eve; or from a woman without a man, which he had never done.

22. Ibid. 1.25.
23. Ibid. 2.6.

So in order to prove that this last way was within his power and had been held in reserve for this very deed, nothing was more fitting than for him to assume the human being whom we are seeking from a woman without a man.[24]

Here it becomes clear that what is most beautiful and 'fitting' is, in Anselm's mind, the same as what is logically necessary, for God will do only what is 'fitting'.

The God-man would then live a perfect life. For one thing, he would have to be perfect, for imperfection would not be fitting. For example, he could not be ignorant in any way, because that would not be useful to his mission. Nor could he ever sin, or else he would owe the debt of sin for himself.

And this would be the whole point of the coming of the God-man: that only he could pay the recompense God's honour required, but which man could not otherwise pay. God needed to be given something that he could not already demand as an obligation. But if the God-man simply lived a perfect life, that would be doing no more than God demands of man. To pay the necessary recompense he needed to do something more, something God could not demand of him. Given the sinlessness of the God-man, God could not with justice demand his death. Thus only by giving his life and dying could the God-man make recompense to satisfy God's honour. Moreover, being God and thus omnipotent, his life could not be stolen from him, meaning he would have to lay it down voluntarily.

At this point Anselm asks Boso if he would be prepared to kill the God-man if that meant saving the whole creation. Horrified, Boso says he would not, and Anselm takes this as proof that the life of the God-man must be worth more than all creation. Indeed, it would have to be, given that the debt man owes to God is worth more 'than everything other than God'.

This is the theology of atonement that Anselm offers in place of the idea of Christ's death as a ransom to pay off the devil. It is not that Christ dies in our place to take any punishment we

24. Ibid. 2.8.

might deserve for sin; it is that Christ's death is an offering to God greater than God could justly demand. It satisfies God's honour, but it does not avert any wrath he might have.[25]

To return to the argument: once the God-man had offered to God the priceless gift of his own death, God's justice would demand that he reward the God-man. Yet the God-man is himself God, and thus would already have everything. It would be impossible to give to him anything that was not already his. So God satisfies his justice by giving the reward to those for whom the God-man died, thus cancelling their debt.

Now if the God-man died for humanity, and the reward amounts to salvation, does that mean all humanity must be saved? Anselm avoids this conclusion by reasoning that God would only offer the merits of the God-man to those who accept the pardon made possible by his death: 'And if they should happen to sin again after this pardon, they will again receive pardon through the efficacy of that same agreement, provided that they are willing to make appropriate recompense and then to amend their lives.'[26]

---

25. It is common for Anselm's atonement theory to be pitted against that of Peter Abelard (1079–1142), the controversial theologian of the next generation. However, just as Anselm is sometimes misinterpreted as holding to a penal substitutionary view of the atonement, so Abelard is routinely interpreted as teaching that, since man could not make a payment to God, and since there was no need to pay the devil, the atonement was not about payment at all, but was nothing more than a moving demonstration of God's love. This was how the enormously influential Bernard of Clairvaux, a staunch defender of the 'ransom to the devil' theory, painted Abelard in his attempt to convict him of heresy. Bernard's logic was that if Abelard did teach that, he would be guilty of Pelagianism (that we need no real reconciliation with God, only an encouragement to be more loving). However, while Abelard did think, like Anselm, that the cross moves us as a demonstration of God's love, he also held to an objective understanding of the atonement. In his commentary on Romans he is quite clear that, unlike Anselm, he held to a penal substitutionary view.

26. *Cur Deus Homo* 2.16.

Why subsequent sin could be atoned for by mere recompense and not by further deaths of the God-man is unclear. What is clear is that salvation was under conditions, and in practice those conditions were tough, requiring absolute submission to the law of God (ideally, becoming a monk).

Anselm and Boso then agree that the logical necessity of the death of the God-man has been proved, and that only through it can the salvation of humanity occur that God's justice required (though angels cannot be saved, for that would require the death of a God-angel). Boso concludes, 'everything that is contained in the Old and New Testaments has been proved . . . you would satisfy not only Jews but also pagans by reason alone'.[27]

Going on with Anselm

When theologically interested Christians consider dipping their toes in Anselm's thought, it is usually *Cur Deus Homo* they go to. Unfortunately, the experience is often rather off-putting, all the to-ing and fro-ing between Anselm and Boso taking up more time than most readers have the patience to endure (*Anselm*: 'Listen.' *Boso*: 'I'm listening.' *Anselm*: 'I will tell you what seems true to me.' *Boso*: 'That's all I can ask of you.' *Reader*: 'Get on with it!'). An easier place to begin is with the *Monologion* (which will also give a better insight into Anselm's overall thought and approach to theology). The translation to use, both for its freshness and accuracy, is Thomas Williams's superb *Anselm: Basic Writings* (Indianapolis: Hackett, 2007), which, as the title suggests, contains all Anselm's basic writings.

Beware of secondary literature on Anselm, which tends to be such that any one book will leave a rather lop-sided impression. The safest hands are probably those of the great Anselm authority, Sir Richard Southern. His incomparable biography, *Saint Anselm: A Portrait in a Landscape* (Cambridge: Cambridge University Press, 1990), gives a beautiful introduction to the man and his mind.

---

27. Ibid. 2.22.

Anselm timeline

1033	Anselm born in Aosta in Italy
1054	Schism between Eastern and Western churches
1059	Arrives at the monastery of Bec in Normandy
1063	Becomes prior of Bec
1066	Norman conquest of England
1075–6	Writes *Monologion*
1077–8	Writes *Proslogion*
1078	Elected abbot of Bec
1079	Peter Abelard born
1093	Enthroned as Archbishop of Canterbury
1095	Pope Urban II calls for the first crusade
1095–8	Writes *Cur Deus Homo*
1097	Leaves England to consult the pope
1098	Defends the Western Church's belief in the *Filioque* at the Council of Bari
1100	King William II of England dies; Henry I invites Anselm to return to England
1103	Leaves England to consult the pope; Henry I forbids his return; Anselm begins excommunication proceedings against Henry
1106	Returns to England with the dispute settled
1109	Anselm dies

6. THE DUMB OX
Thomas Aquinas

Somewhere at the forefront of the medieval mind was the idea that their generation was inferior to the last, that men of old were giants, and medieval thinkers mere pygmies. It was, then, an outlook that gave great credence to 'the authorities', those writings that had come down from grander times. So lofty were they thought to be that, as C. S. Lewis put it, the medieval mind

> hardly ever decided that one of the authorities was simply right and the others wrong; never that all were wrong. To be sure, in the last resort it was taken for granted that the Christian writers must be right as against the Pagans. But it was hardly ever allowed to come to the last resort. It was apparently difficult to believe that anything in the books – so costly, fetched from so far, so old, often so lovely to the eye and hand, was just plumb wrong. No; if Seneca and St Paul disagreed with one another, and both with Cicero, and all these with Boethius, there must be some explanation which would harmonize them.

Or, as he put it more simply, the medieval mind suffered from 'an inability to say "Bosh"'.[1]

That said, particular authorities could go in and out of vogue. Augustine's esteem for Platonism had ensured Plato's pre-eminence right down to Anselm's day; yet soon after Anselm's death a number of works by Aristotle started becoming available to read in Latin for the first time. And Aristotle scratched exactly where the times were itching: where Plato had confined himself to lofty thoughts about the soul and ideas, Aristotle wrote treatises on everything from politics to meteorology to 'the parts of animals', and did so with compelling logic.

Aristotle soon divided the academic world: some seemed to swallow him whole; others saw worrying issues, such as his view that the world had always existed, and decried Christian use of the pagan Aristotle as the sin of Rachel, who smuggled her father's idols under her skirt. How to treat Aristotle became the cause célèbre. Then Thomas Aquinas proposed a system in which he sought to bring Aristotelianism into Christianity in a way that preserved the integrity of both. It would be a Christian Aristotelianism.

The result was triumphant: his masterpiece, the *Summa Theologiae*, became the standard textbook of Roman Catholic theology and was said to have been laid alongside the Scriptures on the altar at the Council of Trent, where he was given the title 'Universal Doctor of the Church'; he was hailed by popes as the 'defender of the Catholic Church and conqueror of heretics'; in 1998 Pope John Paul II issued an encyclical in which he described 'the Angelic Doctor' as 'a model of the right way to do theology'. And his influence has not been confined to Roman Catholicism: even deep in Reformed circles, Aquinas is happily regarded by many as a major influence.

---

1. C. S. Lewis, *Studies in Medieval and Renaissance Literature* (Cambridge: Cambridge University Press, 1966), p. 45.

Aquinas' life

Tommaso d'Aquino was born at some point between 1224 and 1226 in his family castle of Roccasecca, between Rome and Naples. The castle is the giveaway that Thomas came from noble stock. He was, however, the youngest son, and so dealt with in the traditional manner: aged five he was handed over to be educated at the nearby great Benedictine abbey of Monte Cassino, where he soon became known for his repeated question 'What is God?'

After a few years, fighting in the area persuaded his family to transfer him to the new University of Naples, and it was there that he was introduced to two of the great future influences on his life. The first was Aristotle, who elsewhere in Christian Europe was quite unknown (and whose writings were actually banned in Paris). The second was the Order of Preachers ('Dominicans'), an order recently established by Dominic Guzman to combat heresy. Given their intent, the Dominicans gave study an especially high priority, which appealed to Thomas; they were also mendicant friars rather than monks (instead of detaching themselves from the world in a monastery, they lived by begging). Impressed, Thomas soon joined them, and thus entered the Dominican life of study – not study so much for the sake of monastic contemplation like Anselm, but study for the sake of teaching, and specifically university teaching in Thomas' case.

His family were horrified. They had hoped for some high and respectable church office for Thomas, not that he would be on the streets begging with some upstart bunch of radicals. So, when he went travelling north past the family estates, they kidnapped him and imprisoned him for a year or more while they attempted to dissuade him from his chosen career. Dissuasion meant tactics like slipping a scantily clad beauty into his cell to seduce him. Resilience for Thomas meant fending her off with a burning stick (with which he could also make encouraging signs of the cross). Unable to be torn by such distractions from his study of Aristotle's logic and the Bible, he was eventually released.

Thomas headed north to Paris and then Cologne, there study-ing under the great Aristotelian scholar Albert (who was known even in his own lifetime as 'the Great'). Before Albert, nobody really seemed to have noticed Thomas' intellectual potential. Thomas was physically large, tall and portly, and since such heavy features were combined with a distinct lack of personal sparkle, many assumed he was rather backward, and nicknamed him the 'Dumb Ox'. Albert saw otherwise: 'We call him the Dumb Ox,' he said, 'but the bellowing of that ox will resound throughout the whole world.'

Still today, the combination of sharp mind and slow manner make Thomas quite hard to make out. On the one hand, the hagiography has turned the mild-mannered friar into a veritable Buddha of serenity; on the other, his own theological and philosophical output reveal a ferocious intellectual energy. Then there are the anecdotes: in his prime, he would, apparently, dictate to three or four secretaries simultaneously, and would even keep dictating lucidly after he had fallen asleep. There are other stories of his phenomenal ability to concentrate. All told, they seem to suggest a quite remarkable intellectual ability, though it is very hard to know what to believe, since Aquinas' stature as a theologian has steeped his life in legend such that all sorts of miracles and mystical experiences are attributed to him, from levitating to conversing with crucifixes.

Seeing Thomas' ability, Albert arranged for him to return to Paris and study to become a 'master' (a title soon replaced by 'doctor') in theology, even though Thomas was technically too young to be eligible. And so Thomas came to spend his formative teaching years in Paris, lecturing on Peter Lombard's *Sentences* (then the standard textbook of theology), writing treatises and commentaries, and even starting to write one of his major works, his *Summa contra Gentiles*.

After a few years in Paris, he headed back to the warmer climes of his native Italy, and there spent the next decade, half with the papal court, where he became the close friend of two popes, and half in Dominican study houses. It was in one of these houses that he had set up in Rome that he began to write his magnum opus, the *Summa Theologiae*. And from then on, wherever he was (including a stint back in Paris), it was this that dominated, even though he still produced a heavy stream of other works.

He nearly finished it. He had been called back to Naples to set up another study house there, and had just finished writing on the Eucharist. Then, on Wednesday 6 December 1273, while attending Mass, he underwent some profound experience. It so affected him that he never wrote another word, explaining 'I cannot, because all that I have written seems like straw to me.'

The next February, he was travelling to the Council of Lyon, which was an attempt to reunite the Western and Eastern churches, when he hit his head on a tree branch, and had to be taken to the nearby monastery of Fossanova to recover. He never did: there, a few short miles from his birthplace, and still in his forties, he died on 7 March 1274.

Aquinas' thought

Aquinas seems to have spurted ink like a cuttlefish, producing in his short life a staggeringly daunting mountain of books. The definitive edition of his works began to be assembled in 1882, and is still not finished. Fortunately, a good deal of them lie outside the purview of this book – his strictly philosophical writings and numerous commentaries on (all the major works of) Aristotle, for instance.

Biblical commentaries
Among all the collected debates and treatises, some of the most important works are his biblical commentaries (some of which were, apparently, written with the miraculous assistance of the apostles Peter and Paul). In them he developed a highly influential method of interpretation through which he sought to check both the arbitrary manhandling of texts and naive reductionism. Scripture, he held, has two senses: the *literal* and the *spiritual*. The literal sense is about the bare bones of what happens in a passage (e.g. Eli falls off his chair). The spiritual sense is about the meaning of that event, and is a sense usually suggested by another passage of Scripture. There can, however, be three kinds of spiritual sense or meaning: the *moral* or *tropological* sense (e.g. Elijah's prayerfulness is a model for us); the *allegorical* or *typical* sense (e.g. Moses' bronze serpent is a picture of Christ on the cross); and the *anagogical* sense

(about the life to come; e.g. the river Jordan represents the river of death). A passage could conceivably bear all four senses.

Summa contra Gentiles

Yet how can we grasp an overall impression of Aquinas' theology? Undoubtedly, his two greatest works are the *Summa contra Gentiles* and the *Summa Theologiae*. There is, though, a considerable deal of overlap between them, and so, rather than looking at both in minimum detail and suffering the repetition, I will briefly explain what the *Summa contra Gentiles* is, and then we will have the space for a slightly more revealing look at the *Summa Theologiae*.

Traditionally, the *Summa contra Gentiles* (Summary against the Gentiles/Unbelievers) is said to have been written to assist the arguments of missionaries working among the Muslims and Jews of Spain. That situation may well have provided the opportunity for Aquinas to write the work; however, when read, it feels more like an abstract demonstration of what theology can know in distinction to what philosophy can know.

The work divides into four sections or 'books', the first three dealing with what can be known about God from reason: Book 1 discusses what can be known about God from philosophy, especially from the study of Aristotle (who was, if anything, even more influential among Muslims and Jews); Book 2 examines the emanation of creation from God, and Book 3 the return of creation to God. Book 4 then goes on to what can be known about God from revelation (the Trinity, the incarnation, sacraments, resurrection and final judgment). The similarities with the *Summa Theologiae* should soon be obvious.

Summa Theologiae

Written over the last seven years of his life at a speed only Aquinas could manage, and still incomplete, the *Summa Theologiae* is Aquinas' crowning achievement and the mature distillation of his thought.[2] He wrote it, he said, for the instruction of beginners,

---

2. The *Summa Theologiae* (Summary of Theology) is also known as the *Summa Theologica* (Theological Summary).

though since not even friars would have had access to a copy of the work, that probably meant that it was written as a manual for their teachers. Certainly, it was not written for the laity: the *Summa Theologiae* assumes that the reader is quite well versed in Scripture and the theories and practice of scholastic theology.

The *Summa* divides into three main parts: the First Part deals with God and creation; the Second Part deals with humanity's advance towards God in holiness; and the Third Part deals with Christ, the man who is our way to God. The structure can thus be seen to tell the story of God, of how all things come from God in creation, and finally of how all things return to God as they are reconciled through Christ. The endpoint of it all is the resurrection and final glory. Critics have been quick to complain of how Christ is consigned to the final, Third Part. Certainly, it was not Aquinas' intention to relegate Christ in any way – he is treated in the Third Part because he is the one who leads humanity home to God. Yet Aquinas' structure does, of course, have consequences: for one thing, Christ may be shown to be the way of salvation, but he is not really understood as the way to know God.

Aquinas stated that his aim in writing the *Summa* was to convey things briefly and clearly. One is tempted to laugh at his goal of brevity, for, quite apart from the eye-watering page-count (over three thousand in the standard five-volume English translation), he manages to cover questions such as the following: Is there rivalry between guardian angels as to who has the best charge? Are demons influenced by the planets as humans are? Is the soul in each part of the body? Is semen produced by eating too much? Should prayer be vocal? Should Christ have been born in winter? Into which hell did Christ descend, and did he take his body with him? Will we be resurrected with our hair and nails? And will we all be male? Or transparent?[3]

---

3. Fun though it would be to look at Aquinas' answers to these, we simply do not have the time to wander in the side streets of the *Summa* (and, in any case, readers can quickly find them for themselves); my aim is to give an inner sense of the logic and sweep of the work, picking out what is most characteristic of his thought.

Brief the *Summa* is not. But clear it most definitely is. Aquinas'
style is so clear and clean it feels clinical, as if the theological subjects under examination have been scrubbed down, freeze-dried
and then minutely dissected. A good part of this 'feel' comes from
the way Aquinas structures things. He divides his material into
topics, which he calls 'questions'; these topics are then subdivided
into articles. So far that merely feels precise; it is how he then deals
with each article that tends to strike the modern reader as rather
obsessive-compulsive.

Aquinas writes almost as if each article was a transcript of a
medieval scholastic debate. The idea of these university debates
was that, as theologians argued with each other, they would gradu-
ally chip away each other's misunderstandings, enabling them
together slowly to focus in on the truth of the matter at hand.
Thus, as in a scholastic debate, Aquinas opens each article with the
thesis or question to be discussed, objections to it are offered, and
then counter-objections are put forward (introduced by 'On the
contrary').[4] At this point in a scholastic debate the master would
step in with a final response; just so, Aquinas steps in here with
his final assessment of the subject, introducing it with 'I answer',
usually tending to agree with the main thesis, and then dealing with
any outstanding objections. It is the final response that forms the
meat and body of the article.[5]

---

4. Special care is needed when reading the 'On the contrary' section: to our
   eyes today it looks like this is the part where Aquinas' own position is laid
   out. Sometimes it is. But not always. It is the next section ('I answer') that
   should be looked to for Aquinas' final opinion.

5. Given this complex structure, the *Summa* has its own decidedly
   intimidating reference system. Basically, the first number in any reference
   refers to the Part (First, Second or Third); the second number refers to the
   question; the third to the article. So *ST* 3.22.6 refers to the sixth article in
   the twenty-second question of the Third Part of the *Summa Theologiae*. The
   only complication here is that the Second Part actually divides into two,
   which are imaginatively named 'First Part of the Second Part' and 'Second
   Part of the Second Part'. These are referenced as 1-2 and 2-2, making
   ST 2-2.4.5 the fifth article of the fourth question of the Second Part of

First Part

On theology and philosophy The first question Aquinas deals with is
highly revealing. He asks if philosophical reasoning is able to yield
enough knowledge of God to make any other form of knowledge
superfluous. Essentially, his answer is that reason and philosophy
have their place, but can only go so far, and that 'it was necessary
for the salvation of man that certain truths which exceed human
reason should be made known to him by divine revelation'.[6] It
is an answer that will provide the framework for all his theology.
Aquinas holds that reason and natural knowledge provide a foun-
dation on which any supernaturally revealed knowledge received
by faith must build.

Aristotle (whom Aquinas refers to as 'the Philosopher') is clearly
at the forefront of his mind; and Aristotle, he is suggesting, can
generally be relied upon in what he said. However, Aristotle knew
only the natural order of things, which philosophy investigates;
lacking divine revelation, he was ignorant of the supernatural
order, which theology must investigate. Nevertheless, Aristotle
was able to provide reliable philosophical foundations upon which
theology could build. More, despite Aristotle's own ignorance of
the supernatural, his logic was so reliable that it could be extended
to analyse the supernatural realm he had never known.

This model would not simply inform Aquinas' view of how
we know things; it lay at the heart of his notion of reality. There
are two realms, he believed: the *natural* and the *supernatural*, but
the two never conflicted; rather, the supernatural (including faith)
always built upon and perfected the natural (including reason).

---

the Second Part. I will make my referencing no more complicated than
that(!); however, other books on Aquinas do use variations: instead of *ST*
1-2.3.4, one can find *ST* I-II.3.4, *ST* I^a–2^{ae}.3.4, *ST* I^a–II^{ae}.3.4 and more. To
add to the merriment, some like to specify which part of an article they are
referencing. *ST* 1.6.3c, for example: the c is for the corpus or body of the
article, Aquinas' final assessment. *ST* 3.5.3 *ad* 3: *ad* 3 stands for the reply
to the third objection. *ST* 1-2.6.4 *sed contra*: *sed contra* refers to the counter
objection.
6. *ST* 1.1.1.

On the One God What, then, can reason by itself know of God? A good deal, it will turn out:

> The existence of God and other like truths about God, which can be
> known by natural reason, are not articles of faith, but are preambles
> to the articles; for faith presupposes natural knowledge, even as grace
> presupposes nature, and perfection supposes something that can be
> perfected.[7]

But how is it that reason can know of God's existence? Aquinas does not agree with Anselm, that God's existence is hard-wired into our very logic so that if we are logical we have to acknowledge the existence of God. However, he does think that by looking at the world around us we can see God's effects, and that by working up from there we can deduce God's existence. This, in contrast to Anselm's Platonic presuppositions, is itself a very Aristotelian way of proceeding: to start with what can be observed by the senses.

In particular, Aquinas suggests that there are five ways of proving the existence of God from what we know of the world about us. The first (and, Aquinas suggests, the clearest) way works from the fact that we see motion or change in the world. Now everything that moves or changes must be moved or changed *by* something. And, like a series of dominoes, there cannot be an endless chain of movers; otherwise, there would be no first mover and thus no motion or change at all. There must, therefore, be a first unmoved mover, 'and this everyone understands to be God'.[8]

The second way argues quite similarly that there must be a first uncaused cause.

The third way works from the fact that we see things that are capable of not existing. Yet it cannot be the case that everything is capable of not existing, for then at one time nothing would have existed, and nothing can come from nothing. There must, therefore, be a necessary being.

---

7. I.2.2.
8. I.2.3.

The fourth way argues that we see 'more' and 'less' all around; there must, therefore, be something which is hottest, something which is highest, something which is 'uttermost being', 'and this we call God'.

The fifth way is effectively an argument from design, that we see even inanimate things working in ways that seem designed, and so ways that suggest a designer.

These proofs completely lack Anselm's grand ambition of building a complete doctrine of God on an argument. All Aquinas has sought to do with them is establish the existence of a first cause, a mover, a necessary and most perfect being, a designer. In fact, even though he believes we can deduce that God exists, Aquinas is adamant that we cannot know what God is. For Aquinas, we know things by sensing them, but God is not a being we have seen with our eyes, whom we have looked at and our hands have touched; therefore we cannot know God.

This is the point where Aquinas most clearly reveals his reliance on the fifth/sixth-century apophatic theologian, Pseudo-Dionysius (who, in Aquinas' day, was still thought to be the Dionysius of Acts 17, and whose writings were consequently revered as next to canonical). Pseudo-Dionysius had taught – and Aquinas now agrees – that God is such that it is easier to speak of what he is not than of what he is. For example, God is not changeable, for that would imply imperfection (that he had something better to become); God is not bodily, for that would imply that he is somehow spread out in such a way that he can be divided, which is impossible; God is not dependent on anything, even existence.

And yet, if God is so unknown, how can we say anything true about him, wonders Aquinas? Ultimately, then, merely saying negative things about God strikes Aquinas as deficient, especially since he has already 'proved' five positive things about God (that he is a first cause, etc.). Aquinas therefore wonders if, somewhat like Anselm, he should seek to derive an understanding of God from what little we do know of him – that he is the first cause. One could, for example, call God good since he causes good things. But then, he realizes, one could equally call God a nostril or a flea, for he causes nostrils and fleas to exist as well. And, on that track we would remain just as ignorant of what God was eternally like, for was he wise *before* he caused any wisdom to be created?

Yet, because God has caused all things to exist, all things, Aquinas maintains, must resemble him, however weakly. Thus in the end, Aquinas wants to affirm that we can speak truly, if inadequately, about God. We can speak of God, he says, by analogy. That works something like this: if I were to say at one time 'John is an idiot,' and at another 'Rob is an idiot,' I could mean that one of them is merely rather inept while the other is intensely stupid; yet, whatever exactly it was that I meant, you would still have a reasonable grasp of my gist. Just so, when I say 'God is good,' I am not using the word 'good' in exactly the same way as when, for example, I say 'bacon is good'; nevertheless, my basic meaning is clear, for I am using the word in similar, recognizable (analogical) ways.

So we can speak truly of God. What, then, can our reason say, according to Aquinas? Obviously, God is perfect. He is also good – but by this Aquinas is not talking about moral goodness; rather, to be good is to have being. 'Goodness and being are really the same.'[9] This will be an important concept for Aquinas. First, it will mean that nothing can be essentially evil, since being is good; badness is only a lack of being, an incompleteness (thus a bad umbrella, full of holes, lacks the complete being we expect of an umbrella). Second, since Aquinas holds that the essence of goodness is desirability, God, as the supreme being and therefore the supreme good, must be the most desirable being.

What else can reason say? That God is infinite (since everywhere depends on God, he must be everywhere). That God is unchanging (else there would have to be some being prior to him who changed him, making God no longer God). That there is no 'before' and 'after' with God (since time involves change and God does not change). That God is simple, not composed of 'parts' on which he depends.

The next thing about God deduced by reason is especially important for Aquinas: God's knowledge. Aquinas argues that the less material something is, the more free it is to know

---

9. 1.5.1.

things; being completely immaterial, then, God's knowledge must be infinite (which, Aquinas says, is fitting, since intelligence is the highest perfection). Yet Aquinas wants to ask more closely what exactly God knows. Aristotle held that God's infinite knowledge was only of his infinite self – nothing else would be worthy of his consideration. And essentially, Aquinas sounds very similar:

> Since therefore God is outside the whole order of creation, and all creatures are ordered to Him, and not conversely, it is manifest that creatures are really related to God Himself; whereas in God there is no real relation to creatures, but a relation only in idea, inasmuch as creatures are referred to Him.[10]

However, by knowing himself, Aquinas argues, God must know himself as creator, and through that knowledge must have a knowledge of his creation. In fact, creation exists only because God knows it (rather than vice versa). So while God has 'no real relation to creatures', he does have a relation 'in idea'.

The way that works out is that God, who knows and wills what is good (i.e. himself), wills to have beings who reflect his goodness, and he destines them for good (for himself). It is in this way that God loves his creatures. Now at this point it looks like Aquinas is being inconsistent: if God loves his creatures, surely he has a real relation to them? However, by 'love' Aquinas does not mean that God feels affection for his creatures. Far from it; if God could be affected by anything, that thing would have a power over God that Aquinas would consider blasphemously improper. It is, rather, that in all this, God is being true and doing justice to himself. But as he does justice to himself, so he is just to his creatures. The thing is, they do not deserve any goodness or justice from him, and so as he is simply just to himself, so his ways with his creatures can be seen to be merciful.

On the Trinity 'Having considered what belongs to the unity of the divine essence, it remains to treat of what belongs to the

---

10. 1.13.7.

Trinity.'[11] Reason has taken Aquinas so far in his knowledge of God; now he needs revelation to fill in the picture (reason, though, has clearly given Aquinas most of what he wanted to say about God; he is content to be quite brief here). And yet one feels no lurch of a gear being changed here. Aquinas ended his section 'On the One God' by speaking of how God enjoys himself, and this opens the way to a discussion of the Trinity. And, though Aquinas has averred that reason is incapable of discovering the Trinity by itself, reason is quite capable of discussing it, he feels.

Thus the new section flows on smoothly from the previous discussion of God's knowledge: 'whenever we understand', he writes, 'by the very fact of understanding there proceeds something within us, which is a conception of the object understood'.[12] Anyone who has read Anselm's *Monologion* must feel here a certain sense of déjà vu, for this concept now becomes the starting point of a very similar argument. That is, God knows himself, and his concept of himself can be described as a word in his mind, a word that is in God, and yet distinct from God. Next, God loves this concept of himself with a love that is also somehow distinct from himself. And thus there are three in God.

Then, on to each of the three: the Father is described essentially as the principle of the Son and the Spirit; the Son as the Father's concept; the Spirit as the love between them. Their relations distinguish them from each other, and it is for this reason, he holds, that the Spirit must proceed from the Father *and* the Son: if he came from the Father alone, like the Son, then the Spirit would be a second Son.

Aquinas has already explained that God knows himself in his Word, his idea or concept. And 'in idea' he knows his creation. Similarly, the Spirit is God's love for himself, and it is in that love for himself as creator (in the Spirit) that he loves creation.

On creation Having considered God, Aquinas begins to move his story on to consider the creation (of the universe as a whole, of angels, and of man). Medieval theologians are, of course,

---

11. 1.27.Introduction.

12. 1.27.1.

famed for the question 'How many angels can dance on the head of a pin?' There is no evidence that that particular question was ever debated, and yet angels do feature prominently in medieval theology, and first-time readers of the *Summa* are often struck by how much angels figure (more space is given to angels than to the Trinity, for instance). There is a reason, though: angels were perfect subjects for thought-experiments, especially when a theologian was trying to grasp what is true of spiritual beings. He could ask questions about angels that would get him into hot water (literally) if he made God the subject of his enquiry.

Probably the most important section of Aquinas' doctrine of creation is his doctrine of humanity, and this is dominated by his discussion of the soul's relation to the body. Aquinas is emphatically opposed to any sort of dualism whereby the soul and body are construed as two self-contained parts, thrown together. Rather, the soul (*anima*) is the principle of life that animates. I am alive by having a soul. Thus it is not as if I *am* my soul, and that my body is a disposable possession that I could lose without losing myself. Yet nor am I reducible to my bodily functions: I have a life beyond the body. For, Aquinas argues, I think, and that is an activity of the soul.

Now since the soul is capable of acting on its own, the soul must be capable of some sort of independent existence, even after the death of the body. However, it is not so simple as then to say that it is my *soul* that actually understands and thinks. *I* am the one who does that, not my soul. Thus the soul that survives after the death of the body is somehow incomplete and unnatural. That is, Dan's soul, if I part it from his body, is not Dan. And being so incomplete, the soul after death has 'an aptitude and a natural inclination to be united to the body' – by its very nature it awaits re-embodiment and resurrection.[13]

It is with a look at God's providential government of creation that Aquinas ends the First Part, and in it he provides a framework within which much of the rest of the *Summa* will operate. There is, he maintains, no competition between God's

---

13. 1.76.1.

ordering of creation and human free will. Quite the opposite: it is because God wills things that we freely choose them. 'God works in things in such a manner that things have their proper operation.'[14] God is the ground of their being, and so they can only be and do as he allows, but it is not that his will excludes theirs; instead, it enables it. Aquinas' God is a God who enables free will.

First Part of the Second Part
The Second Part of the *Summa* is Aquinas' most original contribution to theology. Having looked at God in his freedom, Aquinas turns here to look at man, the image of God, as in his own freedom he moves towards God. Because Aquinas is dealing here with the 'natural' as opposed to the 'supernatural' realm, he feels able to depend on Aristotle with little alteration (and reveals no sense that Aristotle's God might generate a different world with different ethics to the God of the Bible). The Second Part has thus been described as Aquinas' commentary on Aristotle's *Nicomachean Ethics*; certainly, the argument follows Aristotle's order, though Aquinas knows he must extend Aristotle's logic to examine man's growth in the 'supernatural' realm, something of which Aristotle was ignorant. At points this produces something that just looks rather dated (such as his use of Aristotle's idea that 'the female is a misbegotten male'[15]); overall, though, the result became the definitive Roman Catholic ethic.

He starts with a look at the goal of human life, which, he says, is happiness. All men seek their own happiness where they will. But 'perfect happiness can consist in nothing else than the vision of the Divine Essence'.[16] And how might we attain that? Aristotle had taught that like is known by and drawn to like. Which means that to know God we must be like God; and since God is holy, we must be holy.

On habits Aristotle had averred – and Aquinas agreed – that the

---

14. 1.105.5.

15. 1.92.1.

16. 1-2.3.8.

deep change we need is a matter not so much of our individual actions, but of our habits. Those habits are the tendencies we all have to certain forms of behaviour (whether good or bad), tendencies that are so much a part of who we are that they are hard to break (or form). Such dispositions or aptitudes run much deeper than single actions. For example, one could say 'Reeves is wonderfully athletic': that does not necessarily mean that, right now, Reeves is *doing* something athletic, like running a marathon. Reeves might be sitting at his desk, slurping tea. What it does mean is that whatever Reeves is currently doing, he has a real disposition to long jumps, hurdling and so on.

When Aquinas talks about 'habits', then, he is speaking of something like ethical 'muscle memory', whereby certain behaviour comes more naturally to the person with a certain habit. A good habit is a 'virtue'; a bad habit a 'vice'. To be virtuous – to be the sort of holy person who can know God – one must have virtue, according to Aquinas. But that is a deep thing: one act of virtue will not make a person virtuous, just as one act of vice will not make a person vicious (though repetition of an act will start ingraining a habit). The grain of a person's being runs deeper than single acts, and it is that very fibre of the soul that Aquinas sees must be made virtuous if ever we are to know God.

On law But how, then, can we acquire the virtues we need? According to Aquinas, God gives us two basic forms of help. The first is law, which seems here to be God's fundamental mode of operation. The essential principle of law is that 'good is to be done and pursued, and evil is to be avoided' (note that 'the good' is not about a relationship with God).[17] This principle is built into nature so as to guide our natural aptitude to virtue. On top of this natural law is God's revealed law, both the old and the new. The old law (of Moses) had three parts: the moral, which basically spelt out the natural law; and the ceremonial and judicial, which proclaimed Christ's future work, and thus were annulled when he performed it. The new law (the gospel) has the same purpose as all law, to

---

17. 1-2.94.2.

subject us to God, but with the difference that it is 'instilled into man, not only by indicating to him what he should do, but also by helping him to accomplish it'.[18]

On grace The second way God helps us to acquire the virtues is grace. That is, God pours his love into our hearts, making our hearts lovely and Godlike. This grace is absolutely essential for salvation, for it is not as if I can simply do good things and expect salvation; without grace, nothing I do can be meritorious before God.

Yet when Aquinas came to discuss grace, he found himself forced to disagree with Peter Lombard (c. 1100–1160), author of the *Sentences*, the standard textbook of medieval theology. Lombard had argued that the love of God poured into our hearts is actually the Spirit himself. Aquinas saw this view as hugely problematic, for if that were the case, then not only would our human free will have been violated, but also, it would not really be *us* loving God, but only the Spirit loving God *in* us. But for Aquinas, the whole point of grace is that it is something that changes *us*, that makes *us* virtuous, that enables *us* to merit eternal life. And it is given in such a way that it does not violate human freedom by forcing us to act in a particular way; rather, it is only by co-operation with grace that our dispositions change.

Second Part of the Second Part

Aquinas now proceeds to devote the largest section of the *Summa* to a discussion of the virtues themselves. And here he feels he must go beyond Aristotle, extending Aristotle's scheme into the supernatural realm the philosopher never knew. Aristotle, he holds, knew about the sort of natural virtue that produces a natural human happiness, but since there is also a supernatural happiness of which Aristotle was ignorant, there must be such things as supernatural virtues as well. Once again, Aquinas is showing what little disjunction he sees between the realms of nature and grace. It is as if sin has hardly affected nature at all; grace can simply take nature as it is, extend and perfect it. Certainly, the sense in this Part of the *Summa* is that our problem is not so much sin as lack of grace.

---

18. 1-2.106.1.

On the theological virtues Aquinas, then, starts with the three 'theological' virtues – those virtues that transcend our natural capacities and that can be received only by grace. The first of these is *faith*, which makes the 'intellect assent to what is non-apparent'.[19] Faith, in other words, is that act of the intellect whereby we choose to believe the truths of the church's creeds. Faith, for Aquinas, did not involve anything like personal trust (in fact, none of the virtues is oriented towards personal relationship with God).

The second theological virtue is *hope*, which is the longing for the vision of the divine essence. Hope, according to Aquinas, should not be confused with presumption: only those who persevere in good works can have true hope, and in any case, true hope always involves fear of the loss of what we hope for.

The third theological virtue is *charity*, for which Aquinas takes Augustine's definition: 'By charity I mean the movement of the soul towards the enjoyment of God for His own sake.'[20] There is a sense, however, in which Aquinas understands charity in a vitally different way to Augustine. For Augustine, charity was a heartfelt delight in God; for Aquinas, charity is a quality in the will. This was important for Aquinas, for he saw that if charity is something in the affections, then something must have affected the soul and caused charity to be there. But if that was the case, then charity could not truly be a meritorious product of the soul itself, but must be a response that God could never reward.

Charity, Aquinas believed, is the most important of the virtues, and the root of all merit before God. Without it, faith is nothing but a bare assent that, understandably, could never save. Furthermore, it is charity that makes all the other virtues truly virtuous. 'Charity is said to be the end of other virtues, because it directs all other virtues to its own end.'[21]

---

19. 2-2.4.1.

20. 2-2.23.2, citing Augustine, *On Christian Doctrine*, 3.10. It should not be thought that by 'charity' Aquinas means anything like giving money to the poor, which he would call 'alms-giving'.

21. 2-2.23.8.

On the cardinal virtues As well as the three 'theological' virtues of the supernatural realm, Aquinas taught that the natural realm has its own, entirely valid, virtues. These virtues could be attained by anyone, Christian or pagan, through their own efforts (though on their own they would not be sufficient to save). Chief among them are the four 'cardinal' virtues (from the Latin word *cardo*, meaning 'hinge'): prudence, justice, fortitude and temperance.

Prudence is the virtue without which there can be no virtue, for goodness, according to Aquinas, consists in choosing well. Prudence, then, is the virtue of reasoning what the good is, and then governing the will to act towards it.

Prudence on its own, however, would be impotent, for a whole host of factors always conspires to conflict with what our reason has chosen in prudence. The first, Aquinas says, is that while my will always seeks what is good, naturally it will only seek what is good for me. Yet, somehow, what is good for me is not always what is good for society as a whole. Thus I need the virtue of *justice*, which orients the will towards choosing the common good.

But it is not just the existence of other people that can conflict with my prudence. My own body has appetites that can war against my reasonable choices, and I need other virtues to assist prudence and bring those appetites under the government of my reason. One such appetite is my instinctive desire for self-preservation: naturally, I run from danger, difficulty and death. It is in such situations that the virtue of *fortitude* tells me when to stand up to and endure those things. Another such appetite is my desire for ever more food, drink and sex. Here the virtue of *temperance* enables my reason to govern how much of those things are actually good for me.

While these 'cardinal' virtues belong to the natural realm, and can be acquired by non-Christians, they can also be infused directly into the Christian's soul by God. In this way God can perfect my natural capacities. However, as always in Aquinas, supernatural things only ever build upon natural foundations, and thus, even were God to infuse the virtue of temperance into my soul, if I did not cultivate temperance through natural means, I would remain as vicious, lecherous and gluttonous as ever.

Third Part

Aquinas' aim in the third part was to consider (1) the person and work of Christ; (2) the sacraments by which his work is extended and applied; (3) the final resurrection and last things that his work accomplished.

On the incarnation Aquinas starts with the question of whether Christ had to become incarnate. It was a question he had unique struggles with, struggles highly illuminative of the driving forces in his thinking. Unsurprisingly, he sets out from his understanding of the nature of God, which

> is goodness, as is clear from Dionysius (Div. Nom. i). Hence, what
> belongs to the essence of goodness befits God. But it belongs to the
> essence of goodness to communicate itself to others, as is plain from
> Dionysius (Div. Nom. iv) . . . Hence it is manifest that it was fitting that
> God should become incarnate.[22]

So far, then, Aquinas seems to be saying that God would by virtue of his nature become incarnate – whether or not sin existed.

That said, he feels distinctly uncomfortable with the thought that he might then be constraining God's absolute omnipotence. For, if God is unrestrictedly omnipotent, then the cross cannot have been the way God had to save; if it was, then God's hand would be forced by it. The Almighty must have been free to choose to save the world in another way. In fact, God must have been free to have the Father or the Spirit become incarnate, rather than the Son, or for all three persons to become incarnate in one (presumably rather confused) man; it is even possible, Aquinas feels, that the Son could at some point assume another human nature.

In the end, though, Aquinas feels we simply do not know enough about whether God should have become incarnate, and thus, while our reason suggests that Christ would have become incarnate even had Adam not sinned, the reason he did become incarnate seems to have been that Adam did sin.

From there on, Aquinas' main intention is to show Christ the

---

22. 3.1.1, referring to Pseudo-Dionysius, *On the Divine Names*.

man as the one who exemplifies the standards of virtue laid out in the Second Part. The only virtues Christ did not have were faith (he had knowledge, and so did not need faith) and hope (he already had the union with God that hope desires). And, just as we win merit before God through grace, so, supremely, Christ the man won merit by virtue of the fact that he was actually united to God, the source of all grace. Then, as the exemplary, grace-filled man, he is shown to be the head of the church.[23]

It then remains for Aquinas to look at the actual act of incarnation itself: how Christ took flesh, lived, died, descended to hell, rose and ascended to heaven. This includes a relatively substantial discussion of the role of Mary, who was not immaculately conceived, Aquinas argues, but was sanctified in her mother's womb so that she never committed any sin (making it proper for her to give birth painlessly, live ever after as a virgin, and then be bodily assumed into heaven rather than seeing death). It leaves one of Aquinas' more interesting circular arguments, that through his life and death, Jesus sanctified Mary so that he might live and die.

Aquinas' understanding of the cross is especially significant and illuminative. Like Anselm, he essentially thought of Christ's death as making satisfaction for sin (though, of course, where Anselm saw such satisfaction as necessary, Aquinas did not). Aquinas saw more going on, though: by his death, Christ *acquired merits for us* (as well as freeing us from sin, the power of the devil and the debt of punishment, demonstrating God's love to us and giving us an example of obedience). Thus the cross is made part of Aquinas' overall scheme of salvation by the acquisition of merits.

---

23. Readers of the *Summa* are often struck by the fact that Aquinas does not dedicate any real space to a theology of the church (nobody did until the Reformation). However, Aquinas weaves a quite detailed understanding of the church into his discussion of Christ and the sacraments, and has a large, even cosmic, vision. The church, he explains, includes the Old Testament believers, who 'were borne to Christ by the same faith and love whereby we also are borne to Him' (3.8.3); it also includes angels. We will see more of his ecclesiology as we proceed, though it does remain largely under the surface of the *Summa*.

On the sacraments Aquinas has one, fundamental, governing thought concerning the sacraments: it is that the salvation of the Word-made-*flesh* is given to us through *physical* things. Christ is, as it were, the primary sacrament. He was not just a sign of some invisible grace outside himself. He was and is God acting graciously towards humankind. Thus grace was and is to be found in his very flesh. That, indeed, was the very reason he took flesh: so that through it we might receive grace. Just so, then, the sacraments of the church are not mere signs of some invisible grace outside and somehow separate from themselves; they really contain God's grace within themselves. The sacraments are thus, in a sense, extensions of the incarnation.

It is not, though, as if the incarnation somehow changed things in how God works. God, according to Aquinas, is a God who has and always would work through these sacraments:

> Now, though our faith in Christ is the same as that of the fathers of old; yet, since they came before Christ, whereas we come after Him, the same faith is expressed in different words, by us and by them. For by them was it said: 'Behold a virgin shall conceive and bear a son,' where the verbs are in the future tense: whereas we express the same by means of verbs in the past tense, and say that she 'conceived and bore.' In like manner the ceremonies of the Old Law betokened Christ as having yet to be born and to suffer: whereas our sacraments signify Him as already born and having suffered.[24]

And even in the Old Testament, the sacraments, he argues, were effective: 'circumcision bestowed grace, inasmuch as it was a sign of faith in Christ's future Passion'.[25] And all this is because Aquinas' God is a God who always builds the supernatural (grace) upon natural foundations (bread, wine, water etc.), making it impossible for Aquinas to conceive God ever giving grace other than through physical things.

There are now, he says, seven sacraments. The first is *baptism*,

---

24. 1/2.103.4.
25. 3.70.4.

which washes away our sins and begins the work of transformation in us. Given what it does, baptism is the most necessary
sacrament (though it is just possible to be saved without it – if, for
example, one undergoes the martyr's 'baptism of blood', or if one
desires baptism but cannot have it for some reason). The second
sacrament (dealt with in a blink) is *confirmation.*

The third is the *Eucharist*, and Aquinas' seminal treatment of
it has made him *the* Roman Catholic authority on the subject. To
explain what happens in the Eucharist, Aquinas took Aristotle's
view that each thing has its own 'substance' (inner reality) as well
as 'accidents' (appearance). Then, at the moment of consecration
by the priest, 'the whole substance of the bread is changed into the
whole substance of Christ's body, and the whole substance of the
wine into the whole substance of Christ's blood'. Only the appearance ('accidents') of the bread and wine remain. This miraculous
transformation, he said, 'can be called "transubstantiation"'.[26]
Aquinas meant all this entirely literally: 'By the power of the sacrament there is contained under it, as to the species of the bread, not
only the flesh, but the entire body of Christ, that is, the bones, the
nerves, and the like.'[27] For this reason, he believed, the Eucharistic
elements can and should be reverenced as Christ himself, for they
truly are Christ himself. For all their appearance, they are no longer
bread and wine, but Christ.

As such, Aquinas sees the Eucharist as the crowning sacrament,
for in it God shares himself through the very flesh of Christ. By so
perfectly extending the incarnation, it uniquely encapsulates what
a sacrament is. And, like the incarnation, it is about drawing a body
(of people) together into unity with God. Thus, in many ways,
Aquinas' entire understanding of the church is able to be fitted
into his explanation of the Eucharist, for the Eucharist enfolds the
meaning and reality of the church within itself.

It is, however, a strange irony that, at this very pinnacle of
Aquinas' theology, the scheme we have seen throughout, of the
supernatural building upon and perfecting the natural, has been

---

26. 3.75.4.
27. 3.76.1.

undone. For here the natural creation is annihilated and entirely replaced by another, supernatural substance. Only the husks of the appearance of the original remain. It is enough to make one tremble at the thought of being saved.

Supplement
It was at this point, having just completed his section on the Eucharist, and as he started work on the sacrament of penance, that Aquinas underwent the experience that made him determine never to write again. As a result, he never finished the *Summa*. However, knowing that his intention had been to examine the remaining sacraments (*penance, last rites, ordination* and *marriage*) and then the last things, after his death his students cut and pasted material from his earlier works to fill in what they assumed he would have said.

Going on with Aquinas

Aquinas' style is so dry that he is extremely hard to digest if one bravely tries to read through the *Summa Theologiae*, one article after another; he is, however, so neat and methodical that it is a very easy work to dip into. And he is so lucid that he still makes himself perfectly understood without the need for any great mental effort by the reader (no mean feat after the best part of a millenium). In other words, the *Summa* – which is, quite obviously, the place to get to know Aquinas – is genuinely open to the public.

The best version to use, both for reliability and ease, is the translation by the Fathers of the English Dominican Province. It is freely available online at <http://www.ccel.org/ccel/aquinas/summa> or in print in five volumes under the title *Summa Theologica* (Westminster, Md.: Christian Classics, 1981). There are abridgements available, but the *Summa* is so easy to navigate that they are hardly necessary.

While it is now a little dated, James Weisheipl has written what is still perhaps the most useful single-volume introduction to the man and his thought, *Thomas D'Aquino: His Life, Thought and Work* (Washington D. C.: Catholic University of America

Press, 1974). Two more detailed – and quite brilliant – examinations of Aquinas' theology are Brian Davies' *The Thought of Thomas Aquinas* (Oxford: Clarendon, 1992) and Eleonore Stump's *Aquinas* (London: Routledge, 2003).

Thomas Aquinas timeline

1215	Dominic Guzman founds the Order of Preachers ('Dominicans')
1221	Dominic dies
1224–6	Aquinas born
1226	Francis of Assisi dies
1239	Enters University of Naples
1244	Kidnapped by family en route to Paris
1245	Arrives in Paris
1248	Goes to Cologne with Albert the Great
1252	Returns to Paris to complete studies and begin teaching
1259–64	Writes *Summa contra Gentiles*
1259	Leaves Paris for Naples
1261–5	With the papal court in Orvieto
1265	Opens study house in Rome
1266	Begins writing *Summa Theologiae*
1267	Goes to Viterbo
1268	Returns to teach in Paris
1272	Returns to teach in Naples
1273	An experience leads him to refuse to write any more
1274	Aquinas dies

INTERMEZZO

When Thomas Aquinas died at Fossanova in 1274, the monks there cut off his head and various other body parts to keep as relics. Some years later, they also exhumed his corpse so as to boil off the flesh and keep the bones in a more convenient place for veneration.

Nearly two hundred and fifty years would pass. Then another monk – this time from northern Germany – would set out to oppose the veneration of Aquinas' head. For this monk would like neither relics nor so much of the content of that skull. Directly challenging the now 'Saint' Thomas Aquinas and his use of Aristotle's logic and ethics, he would write:

> Virtually the entire *Ethics* of Aristotle is the worst enemy of grace . . .
> It is an error to say that no man can become a theologian without
> Aristotle . . . Indeed, no one can become a theologian unless he becomes
> one without Aristotle . . . Briefly, the whole Aristotle is to theology as
> darkness is to light.

This monk would not pull punches! There was about to be a revolution in theology.